CHERISHED OBJECTS

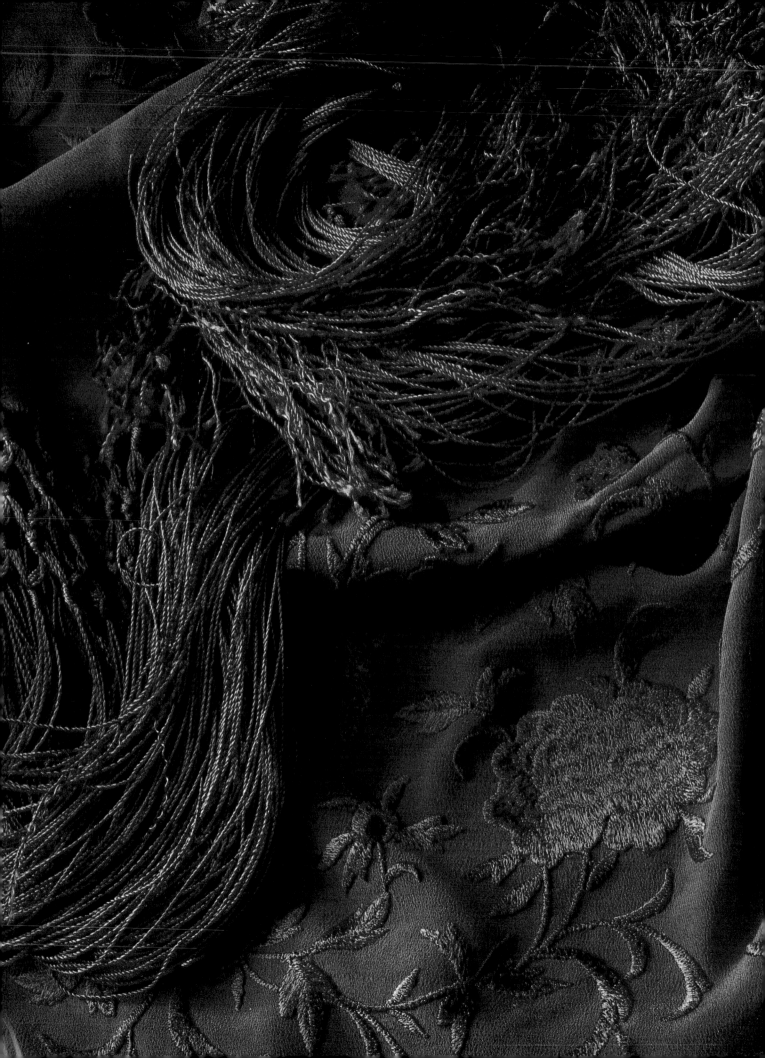

LIVING WITH AND COLLECTING

VICTORIANA

Allison Kyle Leopold

PHOTOGRAPHS BY

Edward Addeo

CLARKSON POTTER/PUBLISHERS

THE REALM OF VICTORIA

1837:

1887:

FOR VALOUR

PER. Nº 378

Published by
Perry & Cº Limited
Steel-Pen Makers
Holborn Viaduct: London:

Entered at Stationer's Hall:

CONTENTS

PREFACE 7

I COLLECTING VICTORIANA...THEN AND NOW 9

1 My Collection—A Personal Point of View 10
2 Collecting Victoriana Today 32
3 The Victorians and Their Collecting 52
4 Arrangement and Display 88

II PORTFOLIO OF HOMES 117

5 Putting It All Together 118
In the Grand Manner 122
In a Nostalgic Way 129
The Country Romantic Retreat 134
The Lure of Victorian Exotica 140
The Modern Mix 144

6 Single-minded Collectors 150
Games People Played 154
Sentimental Journey 158
Citizen Cane 163
Baronial Stronghold 166
Peacock Fever 173

7 Thematic Interpretations 178
Gentleman Jim 182
Object Lessons 191
An Ornamental Aesthetic 198

8 Period-Perfect Collecting 204
Southern Comfort 208
Parlor Games 216

III VICTORIANA DIRECTORY 225

CREDITS AND ACKNOWLEDGMENTS 237
SELECTED BIBLIOGRAPHY AND NOTES 238
INDEX 239

Design by Karen Grant with James Holcomb

Published by Clarkson N. Potter, Inc., distributed by Crown Publishers, Inc., 201 East 50th St., New York, New York 10022. Member of the Crown Publishing Group.

CLARKSON N. POTTER, POTTER and colophon are trademarks of Clarkson N. Potter, Inc.

Manufactured in Japan

Library of Congress Cataloging-in-Publication Data

Leopold, Allison Kyle.
    Cherished objects: living with and collecting Victoriana
 Allison Kyle Leopold; photographs by Edward Addeo.—1st ed.
        p.   cm.
    Includes bibliographical references (p. 238).
    1. Decoration and ornament—Victorian style—Collectors and collecting
—United States.   2. Victoriana in interior decoration.
    I. Title.
NK1378.L46 1991
741.1'09'034075—dc20   90-32621
                                                                          CIP

ISBN 0-517-57435-7

10 9 8 7 6 5 4 3 2 1

First Edition

Quality printing and binding by Toppan Printing Co., Ltd.
  1, Kanda Izumi-cho, Chiyoda-ku, Tokyo 101, Japan.

PREFACE

For those of us who collect Victoriana, it is often the human factor that counts: the style of an object is not nearly so interesting as who owned it, what it was used for, or what it represented to the society that created it. That is why this book, although about objects and about collecting, is not intended as an encyclopedia for technical identification. Instead, it offers an intimate glimpse of the whys, hows, and wherefores of Victoriana, then and now. It is a collection in and of itself of the most intriguing, sometimes endearing, often confusing but always fascinating objects, oddities, romantic keepsakes, curiosities, memorabilia, bric-a-brac, bibelots, and—to go back to a little authentic Victorian terminology—thingums and thingamabobs with which 19th-century Americans liked to surround themselves—as well as a look at those 19th-century objects that continue to give us pleasure today.

In searching out collections for this book, I have been consistently amazed at the creativity, imagination, and knowledge of those people I have come to regard as "my" collectors and how they approach their particular 19th-century passions. It is *their* collections—how they acquired them, display them, how they live with these vital links to our cultural past, some accurately re-creating 19th-century environments, some incorporating them into new interpretations of Victoriana in the 20th century—that have inspired this chronicle of living with objects, a century or more after their time.   A.K.L.

7

Cherished Objects

COLLECTING VICTORIANA
. . . THEN AND NOW

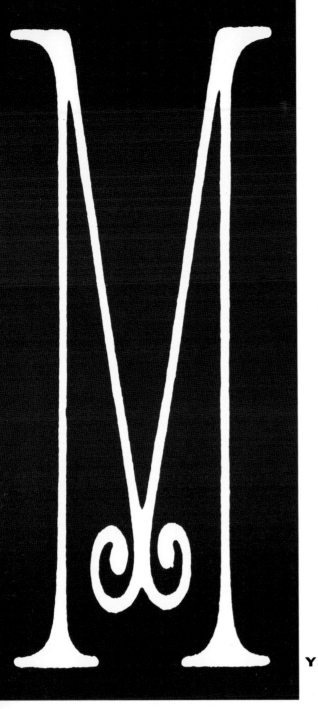

1

My Collection—
A Personal Point of View

People collect for different reasons. Some succumb to collecting fever with investment in mind; others are taken by the thrill of the search, the reward of the find. Sometimes there seems to be no obvious motive; no clearcut understanding of the urge to collect. How does one explain, for

HOTEL BLODGETT

C. E. BLODGETT, PROP.
PERCY TYRRELL, MGR.

DINNER

Celery

Green Sea Turtle
DRESSED LETTUCE, SLICED CUCUMBERS, TOMATOES.

Cutlets of Lake Trout
MONTPELIER BUTTER, POTATOES A LA RIETZ

Boiled Leg Lamb Caper Sauce

Prime Ribs of Beef, au Jus
NEW POTATOES, IN CREAM, MASHED POTATOES

Fried Spring Chicken, Cream Sauce
GOLDEN WAX BEANS, JUNE PEAS

ORANGE WATER ICE

Tenderloin of Beef, Larded aux Mushrooms

Peach Roll Golden Sauce

Lobster Salad

Sliced Apple Pie

Raspberry Short Cake

Vanilla Ice Cream, Assorted Cake

Ice Water Melon

Mixed Nuts, Layer Raisins

American Cheese, Soda Wafers

Tea, Coffee, Ice Tea, Milk

Sunday, Aug. 2, 1903.

Left: **Our parlor, the result of many years of collecting, reflects the spirit, not the letter, of the age. To illustrate the scope of the Victorian century, we've tried to include an example of each of the styles through the successive decades —an Empire teapoy, Gothic Revival and Rococo Revival chairs, a Renaissance Revival parlor set, an Aesthetic Movement étagère, plus oddities like scrap, hair, and shell art; animal-horn furniture; and more.** *Below:* **A clay pot holding an exotic tropical bromeliad is wrapped in an iridescent turquoise silk taffeta, picking up the blues of the 19th-century fireplace tiles. It's held in place with a thick, cranberry-colored cord.**

example, someone's innate response to the taste and style of another century? Somehow, it's been said, one object cries out for others to keep it company. You oblige; soon, you're a collector.

Over the years, people have asked me about my own collecting. Do my personal collections resemble in any way the interiors and collections I see in so many other homes? What objects do I collect; where do my passions, as a collector, lie?

As it happens, it was no easy task for me to answer the questions I've asked of others, to pinpoint the origin of my interest in the objects of 19th-century America—artifacts once useful, once strong and significant in meaning, that no longer play an active part in our daily lives. Without oversimplifying too much, it's an era whose spirit and vigor I like and admire; whose boldness is immediately apparent in the architecture, fashions, art, and artifacts that have come down to us. What I know is I never weary of looking at Victorian objects—they carry with them all the intensity and vitality of their creators.

I collect for one reason and one reason only: delight ... my own private, personal pleasure in a period I find exciting, and romantic, and just quirky enough to keep it all from becoming too serious to live with. My collection isn't grand by any means. Nineteenth-century photographs are among my favorites, even though they are far from rare; they just seem to provoke an inner smile in all who see them (one can only imagine the thoughts that went on beneath those somber clothes and sober faces).

Photography, invented in 1839—just in time to capture the Victorian period—reveals to us people who have not yet learned to dissemble before the lens. Daguerreotypes, tintypes, and other early photographs enable us to "see" the times through Victorian eyes. Differing as they do from paintings and illustrations, photographs provide actual firsthand data, not subjective interpretations. Here is the reality of one hundred or more years ago —how the Victorians' clothing really fit; the way they positioned their furniture; how they embellished their fireplaces; or the types of pictures they hung on their walls. I use photographs to help me "play detective": to probe into the past, to formulate questions, to penetrate the world of century-old objects whose once-familiar purposes are now forgotten.

My feeling of warmth for America's 19th-century Victoriana is unqualified and, some might say, indiscriminate. I like it all. I love the kitchen collectibles —canisters and cake tins, Victorian pie crimpers, pudding molds, the ivory-handled nut picks; elegant, attenuated art glass, with names like peachblow and amberina, and opalescent, iridescent Favrile; juicy-looking blackberry-shaped Victorian buttons; horn furniture; steadfast presentation silver. Perhaps my favorites are the robber-baron furniture—big, heavy, gilded and crested Renaissance Revival pieces, absurdly ornate. To me, their power and bravado trumpet 19th-century values in clarion tones (and no one can tell me the Victorians themselves didn't see some bit of humor in their brashness). At the same time, I also respond to the

Above: **When you enter the hall, you're greeted by "Victoria" and "Albert."** *Opposite top:* **The focal point of the parlor is the mahogany mantel, inset with a collection of antique tiles.** *Opposite bottom left:* **Remnant portions of quilt tops (unfinished quilts) were used to make these crazy-quilt pillows.** *Opposite bottom right:* **A copper washtub becomes an old-fashioned storage bin for the inevitable surplus of magazines, newspapers, and daily mail. Above it, a framed crazy-quilt top produces a stained-glass effect; the Gothic Revival chair to the right is one of a pair purchased at an out-of-town auction.**

more delicate whisperings of Victorian ephemera—fragile valentines, graphic advertising art, old-time magazines, trade cards, menus, calendars—the fleeting bits and pieces of 19th-century popular culture that tell us so much about the common trends and directions of daily life.

As it does to so many of the collectors featured in these pages, Victoriana speaks to me, and I like what it says. Although I am writing this on a computer, it sits (precariously) on a 19th-century library table. When it's time for light reading, I tend to retreat not to the contemporary paperback but to the escape of pulp fiction of one hundred years ago: the silly, sentimental, stereotypical novels— *Thrice Wedded; A Gay Charmer; The Girls of Saint Wode's; Dorothy Dale, A Girl of Today;* and *Polly, A New-Fashioned Girl.* Foolish as they are, they offer a common insight into the way people liked to think of themselves (besides being every bit as entertaining now as they were then).

There is no question that my fascination with Victorian times goes back to childhood. Then, of course, I didn't identify the times as Victorian or 19th century: "olden times" and "dress-up" were the games we three sisters played. To children whose imaginations lead them to make up stories and act them out, the "olden times" they read about in books or see on TV are, in fact, *Victorian* times, set in some nonspecific "long-ago" when girls wore long skirts and petticoats and children scrawled notes on slates in one-room schoolhouses, went on sleigh rides enveloped in fur rugs or woolly hand-woven coverlets. When misfortune befell them, they were, alas, sent to orphanages (or harsh boarding schools) by wicked aunts or unfeeling bank trustees. My first images of these olden times were formed by classic children's books: jolly *Tom Sawyer* (written in 1875), along with *Little Women* (1868), *Eight Cousins* (1874), Frances Hodgeson Burnett's *A Little Princess* (first published as *Sara Crewe* in 1888) and *A Secret Garden* (1911).

I read what Victorian children read—absorbing their culture, identifying with the characters in the same way they did. Although Victorian leisure times were enhanced with enjoyable parlor games and singalongs, a healthy interest in sporting affairs, plus, after 1867, stereoscopes and funny cards to buy and collect, books held the influential place that movies and television hold today (the first, fairly primitive "moving picture" didn't make an appearance until 1890, nearly the end of the era).

Reading was an important part of Victorian life. The world of books embodied the visionary ideals and adventurous spirit that shaped the temperament of the times. After mid-century people basked in a tidal wave of romantic literature and adventures—the Brontës, Charles Dickens, Nathaniel Hawthorne, Mark Twain, Louisa May Alcott, Jules Verne, one after the other—much of it serialized in the magazines of the day. The omnipresent Montgomery Ward mail-order catalogue, catering to a general market in the 1890s, offered more than three thousand book titles to choose from—in a formidable

Opposite: A crazy-quilt top overlaid with scraps of antique lace provides a surface for family heirlooms, including a Jubilee photo of Queen Victoria, 19th-century calling cards, and an old-fashioned "headache" bag filled with sweet-smelling herbs and spices. *Above:* Even ladies depicted in Victorian fashion plates enjoyed a peek at a book. *Right:* The striking similarity of the covers on this collection of popular novels is a clue to the late-Victorian ideal of feminine beauty.

This page and opposite: The fitting out of a linen closet with marked and monogrammed house and table linen was considered a generous gift to a new Victorian bride. Here, thin sheets of rose-colored tissue paper are tucked in between the linens, scented with cinnamon sticks, vanilla beans, and potpourri. Even functional objects had an ornamental elegance; *below,* embossed silver buttonhooks, ca. 1892.

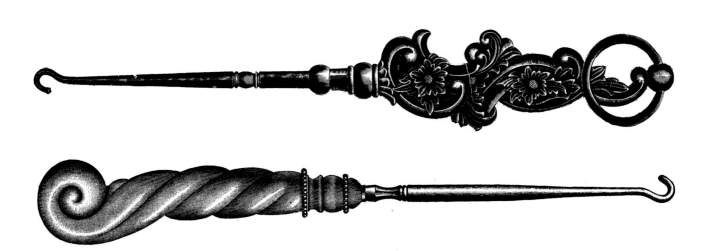

thirty-nine-page section far larger than that for games, toiletries, or women and children's clothing combined. Contemplating the choice of enjoying either *Jane Eyre* or *Wuthering Heights* in the same year was the equivalent of choosing between two first-run hit movies today. Robert Louis Stevenson's *Treasure Island* (1882) was published just two years before Mark Twain's *The Adventures of Huckleberry Finn.* Small wonder the Victorians were the way they were, when their literature was filled with heroes so forthright and certain of themselves and their world, so brash and assured of the truth of their common goals.

As one of a household of girls, probably my favorite book was *Little Women.* It was hard not to identify with one or another of the March girls—each of us was one of those sisters (or all, depending on one's mood)—through one scrape or another. While their dresses might have seemed appealingly dated and quaint, the manners and pastimes described hardly were. Instead, their skating parties and amateur theatricals, their summer picnics and festivities, seemed charming and mannerly and "right"— somehow as "right" as when they were first read by girls back in the 1870s. Stories like these charted in broad, bold strokes my outline of the period's character; years later, I filled in the details.

Everyone garners his or her first impressions of the Victorian era in a different way. Some of us have been seduced by romanticized tales of life in the Old South—the images of those wonderfully romantic ball gowns in *Gone with the*

Left: The view from our kitchen, looking through old-fashioned pocket doors into the dining room, at holiday time.

Above and opposite top: An overview of the dining room, the table set for dessert. Contemporary placemats are used over an antique lace cloth; the napkins are from my collection of vintage linen. The Limoges dinner service (ca. 1922) belonged to my husband's grandmother. A Victorian silver bell and a collection of 19th-century menu ephemera (close-up, page 11) surround the centerpiece. Tiffany silver salts are filled with marzipan and chocolate candies. The "family" portrait on the far wall is a modern primitive by Barbara Philips.

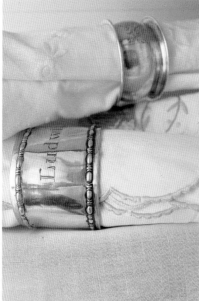

Above and above right: **To keep laundry work in check, Victorians tried to use the same napkins for several meals, neatly folding the squares and tucking them into personalized napkin rings marked with either their names or initials. Some napkin rings had scrolled or engraved borders; others, elaborate, figurative subjects (children, pets, animals, flowers, or fruit motifs). The whimsical nature of the latter tells us they were used for family meals, rather than for formal occasions. This collection of antique napkin rings, glinting in a bowl in the kitchen, creates a holiday mass of silver the Victorians would have been proud of.** *Preceding pages:* **A collection of vintage tins, displayed on the kitchen counter.**

Above: **Photos of children along with a hand-colored print of a 19th-century furniture showroom and a wonderful framed French theater magazine make even the bathroom a collecting showcase.**

Wind, with billowy skirts of glistening taffeta and froths of lace. In the 1950s and 1960s scores of popular TV westerns featured Victorian lamps, rugs, beds, tables, and chairs as Wild West furnishings. *Bonanza, Gunsmoke, The Wild Wild West, Maverick, Bat Masterson, Wagon Train*—all are Victorian in decor. Watch reruns of any of these classics and notice, this time around, the Victorian frills— the hanging lamps and marble-topped tables, the fringed pillows, the towering Renaissance Revival beds and bits of Victorian wallpaper.

Like many collectors, I found my way into collecting Victoriana through the back door, so to speak—through the solid, mass-produced, golden-oak pieces popular in the closing years of the Victorian century. Sturdy, glowingly golden, and appealingly old-fashioned in a casual country Victorian way, they had—and still do—a sense of comfort and permanence. During the 1890s and through the turn of the century, young Victorian Americans took to the simplicity of the round oak pedestal tables and pressed-back chairs, the dependable oak washstands and cabinet pieces.

As for my husband and me, these were the first "antiques" we discovered as newlyweds when we were looking for affordable furniture for our first apartment. How we agonized over those early purchases: a tall oak china cupboard with glass doors and brass hardware; a tiger-striped oak library table; a five-drawer dresser with a feminine, curving front and oval mirror. Most of these pieces we still own today.

By the time we moved to our present home, in a building that dates to 1882, our interest and level of collecting 19th-century furnishings had expanded and deepened. We embraced this new passion with fervor: for the rich, historical associations, and for the very Victorian pleasure of owning something unique, one-of-a-kind. Soon our tastes turned to more formal 19th-century furnishings—walnut, rosewood, and mahogany—as well as to the full range of curiosities and collectibles. A favorite early keepsake was a 19th-century valentine, whose hand-scripted verse contained an audacious marriage proposal from a love-lorn mid-Victorian Romeo in the last line.

My love, vain are words here to relate,
The pleasures of a wedded state.
With anxious eyes here gaze;
Mark the sweet composure of the bride.
This in example, let her be your guide.
Unite with me to dwell in Hymen's maze.

No question, we were hooked: the living room was slipping further back in time, looking more like a "parlor" every day. Much of our original golden oak moved to the guest room, family room, and nursery. Unlike many collectors, I "trade up" only on occasion—preferring instead to shift things, move them around. Recently we sent some golden oak up to our family's early Victorian (ca. 1840) farmhouse, in *Legend of Sleepy Hollow* country. There, combined with country finds and family hand-me-downs, this informal collection of Victoriana seems at home.

Shifting old-fashioned, out-of-date, or less showy furnishings from the

Top: An early-Victorian framed valentine that actually contains a marriage proposal in the verse. *Above:* A 19th-century silver-topped inkwell, a bit of fringe, and the famous Elsie Dinsmore series are the components of this vignette.

parlor to more private rooms of the house, by the way, is a custom well rooted in Victorian tradition. During the 19th century, when the parlor or the drawing room was a showcase for only the newest and the best, older, less fashionable articles of furniture were frequently assigned to a back bedroom or other less visible room of the house upstairs. In a typical home of the 1870s or 1880s, for example, one might have found grandmother's old wing chair, possibly in need of re-covering, no longer suitable for the front parlor but still homey and comfortable, sitting cozily in the corner of a spare bedroom.

Through the years, different objects have caught my eye, and I've gone through several stages as a collector. As with most novices, I had trepidation about my first "serious" purchase, nervously writing a check for a beautiful 19th-century center table that represented a collecting milestone for us, immediately outshining all the other furnishings in the room. And, as is always the case, once the plunge is taken, subsequent major purchases, unfortunately, come all the easier. We knew then we had made the leap.

Years later, we discovered that table was by Herter Brothers, whose works are among the most sought after by collectors today. Over the years, though, I've made my share of mistakes, sometimes at auction, where, by way of a hesitant hand or heart, I've let some prize slip by. I still remember—regretfully—a certain Victorian pedestal I passed up at an unexpectedly heated country auction when my judgment—or perhaps courage

—failed. Then there was the time I attended another auction with a dear friend, also a passionate "Victorian." Holding back, each of us anxious to avoid bidding on a velvet-covered Rococo Revival chair we were sure the other wanted, we both lost out to another, less polite bidder.

Fifteen years ago, when Victoriana was still undercollected, it was fairly easy to satisfy the collecting urge at country auctions, flea markets, and fairs; even to pick up small collectibles for as little as a dollar or two. Now, much of what we admire have become unaffordable passions: the Belter settee, Tiffany glass, Aesthetic furniture, Handel lamps. Yet, because of the duration of the era and the enormous variety of things produced from the late 1830s through 1915, most collectible Victoriana is, thankfully, still within reach at antiques shops, auctions, estate sales and fairs, flea markets, and even yard sales (not to discount the occasional happy attic find). Victorian collectibles have passed the testing point, and more treasures are recognized and uncovered every day.

My collection now is a combination of new and old, family pieces, fortuitous finds, and special acquisitions. Far from a period-perfect interior, it is, as were the contents of the original Victorian homes, a medley, a mixture, a personal assortment. My preference is for Victorian things —whether the prize of a museum-quality table or the anomaly of a gilded tramp art frame—that have a story to tell, a tidbit of information about the period to impart.

Opposite: **Three of the bins in this early Victorian teapoy hold fragrant tea leaves, the fourth, telephone message pads and pens. The top provides a place for a collection of odd, unrelated smalls, including a 19th-century ivory game spinner, a souvenir pin cushion, and an antique magnifying glass. The late 19th-century Shakespeare,** *above,* **serves both as letter opener and bookmark.**

Victorian craft pieces of all kinds also intrigue me and are worth seeking out. By "craft," I mean those handworked home embellishments that represented so many hours of 19th-century women's lives —linens and embroidered lace—as well as handicrafts peculiar to the time— shellwork, hair art, moss pictures, découpaged scrap screens. Crazy quilts—tops and fragments, plain and fancy—have a special place throughout our house. One skirts a round table with its colors; another, an unfinished quilt top, is framed on a wall. Fragments, when repaired, have a new existence as parlor pillows.

As I travel and meet with collectors across the country, I've observed many different ways to incorporate Victorian antiques and collectibles into the home, often based on time-honored 19th-century traditions. Some, I've managed to bring into my own home. On these pages are a few of my favorites.

Most of my collection, with a few exceptions, is intentionally American in origin, although I'll bend a bit and collect something from England, or from France, if I feel it's something Americans of a century ago would have owned or responded to. Basically, though, it's the distinctly American feel of 19th-century antiques and artifacts that attracts my sympathies and eye. While Americans looked to European design movements for inspiration, they interpreted it all with a clearly American spirit. What flowed from the hands of Victorian American craftsmen and through the doors of the first factories was freer, looser, more robust— as were the Americans of that time. In-

Above and right: **A collection of 19th-century physician's letters, bought at auction, along with silver desk accessories.**

Above: **This precious little one enthroned on a late-Victorian wicker chair is doubly special because of the simple—but gilded—tramp-art frame. The sober-looking Union soldier encircled in shellwork was found in New England.** *Left:* **This serpentine-front turn-of-the-century golden-oak dresser, now in a guest room, was one of the first pieces we collected.**

stead of merely duplicating European models, they adapted the look to the American landscape, its life and developing sensibilities. And how it all changed! Designs attuned to the European handmade tradition were modified or replaced by ones suited to the precision and inventiveness of the machine, which had so much to do with the look of American Victoriana. The exciting capability of working with hardwoods like walnut and oak, the sturdier construction and fit, even the flamboyance and abandon with which pieces could now be ornamented—all are by-products of the Victorian machine age.

Not to be underplayed, either, is the strong, national pride reflected in American Victoriana. *Being* American was important in the 19th century. Furniture, objects, technology—all were the exuberant progeny of a young country on its way to becoming the center of the world. This was especially true after the Centennial of 1876, which celebrated, with its bountiful exhibits of things and more things, the culmination of one hundred years of American progress, as well as the independent spirit that inspired it.

And all of this contributes to the attachment felt toward the Victorian century, the natural affinity we seem to have with its style. It is a comfortable style and Americans today are comfortable with it, at home with its heritage and essence, and its endearing pretensions. And why not? As the first truly American style, it was born of the American spirit—far more Teddy Roosevelt than Marie Antoinette.

Left: Salesmen's samples were miniatures of full-sized furnishings used by salesmen to demonstrate the quality and style of the goods they were offering. This "sample" dresser sits atop an antique pine child's cabinet draped with lace. The brown and white china "jug" is a Victorian transfer-printed toothbrush holder.

Left and opposite: Scrap screens, composites of beautifully and eclectically arranged bits of Victorian scrap (a popular collecting pastime in the second half of the 19th century), were perhaps the ultimate expressions of the layered look the Victorians indulged in to the fullest. This particular screen (ca. 1880) was probably created for a nursery.

2

COLLECTING **V**ICTORIANA **T**ODAY

More so perhaps than any other cultural period, the Victorian era cherished objects. Victorians conceived of them, produced them, acquired them, and displayed them with an enthusiasm unfettered by any of today's self-consciously tasteful restraints. Between 1860 and 1900, more than

676,000 patents were granted by the U.S. Patent Office, with 26,272 patents filed in one year (1890) alone. In furnishing a home, if one teapot was good, two were better, and three, four, or five a positive delight. In 1884, Montgomery Ward's mail-order catalogue brought the tantalizing choice of more than ten thousand objects into the home; by the mid-1890s that selection had more than doubled. Yet, looking at 19th-century "object lust" from a Victorian sensibility, it is no surprise that this carnival of accumulation took place. In the pre-Victorian era (the first quarter or so of the 19th century) even the most basic goods were scarce; purely decorative or art objects were in reach of the wealthiest classes alone. A scant fifty years later, prosperity, invention, and leaping advances in technology had materially improved American life. A fantastic array of goods existed where once there were none—as did the ready money with which to buy them. There were practical inventions like Mrs. Mary Florence Potts's 1872 cold-handle "sad iron" ("sad" being the archaic word for "heavy"), a boon to homemakers and used for smoothing and polishing shirt fronts. There was the parlor stove, with sparkling decorative chrome; Mr. Singer's sewing machine; the first paper dress pattern (a significant breakthrough, since most dresses were made at home for nearly the entire span of the century); along with the electric light, phonograph, and telephone. There were also a thousand and one utterly Victorian but seemingly necessary trifles: from egg-shaped glass hand coolers (used to refresh a lady

From the glory of a fine oak heater (ca. 1902), *below,* sparkling with decorative chrome (advertised for $9.30 in *The Ladies' World* as "faultless" and "the best in the world"), to Victorian silver, one of the more glittering examples of 19th-century "object lust." The proliferation of beautiful, highly ornamented domestic items such as these, *opposite,* marked the Victorians' newly awakened taste for the accoutrements of civilized living, and they brought opulence and elegance to the table at affordable prices.

hard at work on a laborious needlework project) to a Victorian clockwork fly-swatter machine with handy cloth-covered paddles to keep guests cool and shoo away flies at the same time. Ladies delighted in novelty perfume vials the shape of a lady's slipper. And how fine it was to start the day with one's own three-piece *imported china* "mush and milk set" (cream pitcher, plate, and bowl) with its "handsome flower decoration in their natural colors" reassuringly warranted by the manufacturer not to wash or wear off.

For many Americans, often just a generation away from the grim struggle of the frontier, where one's possessions might include a cow, a cup, a hand-hewn table, a straw-filled bed cover and bedstead, and little else, this abundance of things created the Victorian equivalent of the kid-in-the-candy-shop syndrome. There was justifiable pride and satisfaction in a handsomely turned out parlor, with lambrequins draping the windows, fine plaster statuary and wax flower wreaths, the whatnot in the corner brimming with curios and collectibles. A passage in the popular Victorian novel *Marcia Schuyler,* set in 1831 but written from the worldly vantage point of 1908, illustrated the feeling: "You ought to be very proud to have a husband who could buy a thing [a piano] like that." This from an elderly aunt chiding her nephew's new bride. "There's not many has them. When I was a girl, my grandfather had a spinet, the only one for miles around, and it was taken great care of. The case hadn't a scratch on it."

The glory of the Victorian age

was a look of hard-won plenty, joyfully announcing just how far we had come—the sprawling pattern of a new Brussels carpet blossoming with pneumatic roses, warming once-bare floors; windows hung with layers of tasseled plush (double-faced and in "rich Paisley designs in olive, gold, blue or cardinal," but 19 cents a yard, in 1895). And there were lavishly patterned wallpapers—they gave one plenty to look at in places where those clever Currier & Ives prints weren't already covering every inch of available wall.

Victoriana—the simple, everyday artifacts of daily 19th-century living, the precious family heirlooms, the choice keepsakes, the opulent antiques, the sin-

Vintage dance cards, *above,* **and a beribboned tussie-mussie (a nosegay carried in a delicate silver holder),** *opposite,* **evoke the life and charm of the era.**

gular curiosities of America's 19th century—does indeed have a special hold on the contemporary imagination. Created by people who revered abundance as an expression of their taste and desires, these objects have an intensity that holds fast today. Reaching out to us across the span of well over a century, they spur a store of half-forgotten memories.

The best collections of Victoriana (or of anything, for that matter) are those that spring from a strong emotional response, either to the aesthetic of the object (i.e., the beauty of a fine 19th-century quilt can easily be compared with that of a painting) or, more frequently and more tellingly, to the historic background that object carries with it. For example, the

truncated half-arms on what the Victorians called ladies' chairs, standard pieces in Victorian parlor sets, resulted not from a misguided sense of proportion but rather as an accommodation to the full, crinolined skirts of the 1850s and 1860s. On these chairs, with their oddly abbreviated arms, a lady dressed in voluminous hoop skirts could perch with some semblance of comfort.

Social conventions and fashions also contributed to the oddities, the novelties the century produced. Late-19th-century mustache cups, for instance—porcelain or pottery mugs sometimes adorned with hand-painted forget-me-nots or inscribed "Father"—examined from a purely aesthetic sense, are fairly mundane objects, except for the little inner ledge on which a gentleman's prized mustache could safely and dryly rest. What makes them a temptingly collectible slice of the past (above and beyond their admittedly minimal aesthetic) is the wealth of information these simple cups impart about 19th-century culture. Their very existence emphasizes the pride with which mustaches of operatic proportions were cultivated. "It is the mark by which God meant that men and women should be distinguished," wrote the venerable Timothy Titcomb, Esquire, in his letters "to young people, single and married" (1858). Since, during the 1860s and 1870s, the inability to grow facial hair was considered a sign of effeminacy, men frequently sported luxuriant, walrus-style mustaches—hardly practical appendages. Approvingly noted in the memoirs of one lady was her sister Bea's exemplary

The Victorian mustache cup, *above,* **a staple of the 1890s, is a collectible curiosity today.**

fiancé, "Brother George," who had a "crisp, well-behaved little mustache and never used a mustache cup at table."

Throughout the second half of the century, though, these fanciful mustaches prevailed. With the approach of the new century, however, the clean-shaven look began to be favored (brought about in part by the popularity of handsome, smooth-cheeked journalist and man-about-town Richard Harding Davis, whose late-Victorian good looks marked him as something akin to the masculine equivalent of the Gibson Girl). The result: mustaches—and with them, mustache cups—gradually disappeared.

Because of its rich, evocative store of tales and associations, bygone customs, and tradition, the Victorian century has a strong fascination for us today. These associational aspects—preserving some record of the pattern of life of the previous century; telling us what people wore and why they wore it; what they enjoyed reading; how they walked, talked, cooked, courted, traveled; how they raised their families and spent their leisure hours—are key to the appeal of Victoriana today.

Even the word *Victorian* conjures up images of the well-cherished objects that filled the home, domestic objects that the Victorians enjoyed and that retain their associations with the era today. Cupboards of china, painted with peonies and primroses; silver serving pieces; old-fashioned card cases; dressing-table accessories with ornate handles worn smooth over time—these objects and more (always with Victoriana, the key is more), clustered on tabletops and mantels, tucked into niches, perched on pedestals and covering every inch of quaint little shelves, *cherished objects,* were the heart and soul of the American Victorian home.

As the century progressed, the Victorians' innocent pride in these objects was complicated by an increasing preoccupation with etiquette, status, and social class (one of the traits of the Victorian character was an ingrained need to "improve" oneself morally, socially, and intellectually). As a result, the home and its furnishings gained a crucial social significance. "Mrs. Derling, you look as though you could give a room an *inhabited* look —a look as though the occupants were people of culture and refinement, and capable of appreciating the poetry of life; will you take this room in hand?" asked Mr. Cliverford in "Mr. Cliverford's Strategy," a short story published in an 1866 issue of *Peterson's* magazine. The widowed Mr. Cliverford, having engaged Mrs. Derling as housekeeper, was at the same time eyeing her for the more elevated position of wife. Her success or failure at decoration was unquestionably an indication of her character and values. Objects, those for home decoration in particular, had begun to assume an importance far beyond that of either aesthetics or practical function (Mrs. Derling's efforts, by the way, which included the addition of "exquisite brackets, fashioned by [her] own hands from acorns and shells and segar [sic] boxes" met with the awed approval of Mr. Cliverford and his family and neighbors). In the new, striving soci-

A sugar bowl (ca. 1884) became more useful when outfitted as a spoon holder, *right.*

Few items have more potent social history than 19th-century mourning memorabilia, *this page.* The relief-sculpted memorial cards, black-bordered stationery and certificates (the collection *above* even includes a leaf from Queen Victoria's funeral wreath) remind us that the reality of death was far more integrated into the cycle of Victorian daily life than it is today.

ety of the later Victorian decades, things became representative of their owners in a very literal way: evidence not only of one's character and connections, cultural aspirations and taste, but frequently as a measure of morality as well. In this Horatio Alger world, prosperity was considered a sign of divine approval; misfortune, the reverse. In such a society, is it any wonder that people often became obsessed with frantic accumulation? Laden with weighty and telling social significance, objects were carefully chosen— and just as carefully scrutinized.

It is Victoriana's strong social and personal connotations that have brought it into its own as highly collectible, appealing to a broad range of enthusiasts. How collectors savor those past-century bonds!—smooth oval boxes of wood or tooled leather, which, when opened, might still contain a collar or two, nestled inside. The charm of a little slipper chair grows dearer when one remembers it made the lacing and unlacing of high-button shoes a little easier. Once one understands the secret language of Victoriana and can break its code, the messages these objects carry speak eloquently to us about the domestic habits of bygone days. It is that appreciation for the connection of the object to its times —as T. S. Eliot put it, for objects as cultural emissaries—that sets collectors of Victoriana apart.

The term *Victorian* is best defined not as a style of architecture, a type of furniture, or a mode of decorating but as an era—from roughly the 1830s to the start of World War I—marked by com-

The traditional sideboard, filled with primrose-patterned china, was once an emblem of domestic prosperity.

mon attitudes, beliefs, and behavior. (To equate the end of the Victorian era in America with either the end of the century or the death of Queen Victoria [1901] is convenient, but hardly accurate. During the first years of the 20th century, manners and customs and way of life barely changed: proper Victorian mores lingered, happily, easing only slightly throughout that gentle decade, the magic charm of those peaceful years broken only by the rude advent of war. Just as forty years earlier the upheaval of the Civil War abruptly ended a long-established way of life—and an era—so again, it was war that disrupted America's Victorian expectations and attitudes, plunging us headlong into modern life. For all practical purposes, *Victorian* refers to that period of time that loosely—very loosely—corresponds to the reign of England's Queen Victoria [1837–1901], adjoined with that of her son King Edward VII [1901–1910].)

This period, encompassing most of the 19th century, was a self-assured time in our history, a time of exuberant expansiveness and growth. Cities flourished where once there had been only small towns; thriving towns and villages sprang from prairie outposts and frontier settlements. A large agrarian nation became an enterprising urban one. Railroads snaked across the country, binding it together in a complex web; roaring steam engines thrilled the crowds. Crinolines came and went; bustles and hourglass corsets took their place and reshaped the feminine silhouette. Improved methods of communication (of every sort,

The sweetly sentimental decorative sensibility and taste so prevalent at the end of the century can be seen at a glance in this still-intact calendar.

from penny newspapers to telegraphs and finally telephones) spread the news to a populace of increasingly diverse backgrounds, as generation upon generation of immigrants poured into the new nation, refueling its energies and ambitions. It was a time when invention, innovation, and opportunity were ripe. And when, as legend has it, Pierre Lorillard, a manufacturer of snuff and tobacco, died in 1843, leaving an estate of over a then-monumental one million dollars, it was the Victorian era that introduced a thrilling new word to America—*millionaire*.

In contrast to the frenzied activity of the outside world—and perhaps because of it—daily life became increasingly home-centered. The home emerged as a retreat, a haven of security and familial warmth, far from the undeniably stimulating but still confusing flurry and bustle of worldly life. The Victorians were drawn to the natural excitement of progress, irresistibly aroused by the creative innovations of their times. As the century raced by, it seemed a chronicle of giant steps to the future with its whirlwind of historical events and technological advances turning the fabric of daily life inside out, with gleeful Victorian gusto.

What a heady time it was! Even seemingly mundane achievements caused wonder. The luxury of actually owning a machine-made(!) lace collar (not one clumsily worked at home); the miracle of store-bought wood floor planks—planks amazingly smooth and, even better, all the same size (so fine compared to irregular old-time logs). These were things worthy of note to settlers in the Dakota

The quirky charm of footstools, *above,* and the country calm of the porch, *right,* are both symbols of Victorian comfort—efforts to fashion 19th-century homes into havens of security. *Overleaf:* The rich and provoking faces of those who inhabited the era are complemented by the variety of fanciful frames, in this collector's cache.

Childhood collectibles, from vintage toys, *above,* to heirloom portraits, *right,* testify to the important place children held in the 19th-century world.

territory during the 1870s. The marvel of a schoolhouse patent desk "made of wood [but] varnished as smooth as glass" particularly impressed one girl used to the rough-hewn logs and more rustic furnishings typical of frontier living, enough to fondly set it down, forty years later, in remembrances of her girlhood. Remarking on the fact that one of her enterprising townfolk had plunked down a heaping sum of money for one of those new sewing machines—well, why not? "There's no flies on Clancy," approved a neighbor. His enterprise was to be admired, not sanctioned.

At the same time, the cultural turmoil wrought by such changes frightened and confused people. Economically, technologically, and politically, Victorian Americans hurled themselves forward, assured of their right, recklessly proud of their success and the abundance it was creating. Domestically, though, they shrank back, as if longing for the simple life of the idyllic green countryside, now rapidly disappearing. In 1889, the community of Guthrie, Oklahoma, quite literally sprang up overnight. What was on April 22 a sleepy section of Indian territory was transformed on April 23 into a bustling tent city of more than 10,000 inhabitants as the land opened for settlement. A mere five days later, the construction of stores and buildings, false fronts and all, was already under way.

Things seemed to be moving, changing so fast. For many, the headlong replacement of the old with the new was creating a discomfiting world. It was as if, along with the clanking industrial

Below: **The comfort ethic, as displayed in this engraving from *Harper's Bazar* (1883) of an inventive rocker cozy with padding, embellished with embroidery and heavy with fringe.** *Overleaf:* **Past-century bonds . . . in well-worn collar boxes, in cherished valentines. . . .**

noises and soot of the new age, progress also generated a jittery emotional debris. It was out of this unease with modern life that the Victorian home as we know it emerged, a cluttered cocoon, a warm haven, a retreat.

The ideal Victorian home tended to boast a parlor that see-sawed clumsily between homely comfort and happy grandeur: its thickly upholstered chairs with well-padded backs, cozy fringed footstools, and recliners draped with colorful shawls contrasting sharply with tall, sumptuously curtained windows topped with swagged velvets, looped festoons, and lavishly trimmed brocades. Floors, copiously carpeted—an Oriental rug perhaps layered over boldly patterned wall-to-wall—increased the feeling of a protected, womblike enclosure. With its rich, rustling masses of fabric, objects, and treasures loading the tables and mantels (a bounty of new things to admire), the whole was rich, warm, deeply satisfying, despite an admittedly edgy undercurrent.

The public rooms of the Victorian home—the parlors, dining room, and entry hall—were the main receptacles of fulsome Victorian display—public pronouncements of the 19th century's self-made new-found prosperity. Quite naturally, they were also the rooms where most of the objects and collectibles that the Victorians accumulated found a home. The carefully decorated hallway, for instance, was designed to create a dignified, solid—and fast—first impression. Crimson and gold, more likely than not, were the colors that fit the bill. But every color, every pattern, every bit of hallway deco-

With my love

ration—from the deep, impressive tones of the wallpaper to the gleam of brass carpet rods on the stairway—were chosen, usually after thoughtful deliberation, for definite and contrived effect. A proclamation of status, an inviting preface to the rest of the home, the sober splendor of the hallway set the tone for what was to come. And what was to come was just as carefully considered.

In the parlor, or drawing room, the subtleties and intimations of the hallway were banished, replaced by a swaggering, full-blown, triumphant collision of luxury, culture, and ornament, mixed, for good measure, with a little down-home domestic handiwork. In this room, a true reflection of Victorian pride at its height, objects were assembled not only as evidence of material wealth but, just as important, as confirmation of aesthetic appreciation, strictly interpreted (and then, easily understood) symbols of taste. Porcelains, statuary, paintings, the most up-to-date furniture and carpetings, an étagère laden with all sorts of treasures (so practical too, Victorians thought, to stir up interesting and erudite conversation)—these were the staples of the innocent excesses of the room.

The parlor promoted the level of aesthetic taste of its owners; the dining room contained objects of a different nature entirely. Here an atmosphere of solidity and tradition ruled; here furnishings were chosen with more stately purposes in mind. The dining room was deep-toned, sober but not somber. The dominant impression of its furnishings and the choice of its significant

Artifacts and curiosities of exotic or educational bent focused conversation, helping guests avoid "common" talk of dress or scandal (gossip). The ebonized étagère holding collectibles and this side table display in our parlor, *above*, are typical of the custom. Family pride as well as a fascination with novelty inspired Victorians to fill their homes with portrait photographs like these, displayed in a collector's home today, *opposite*.

objects satisfied the Victorian need for visible expressions of family heritage and prosperity. A visually warm room, sometimes leaning toward the baronial, the parlor often featured a gallery of family portraits (or lithographs with images of fruit, fish, and fowl that the Victorians clearly labeled, lest there be any confusion, "dining room art"). And, of course, there was the long, heavy dining table, blanketed in snowy damask, flanked by a regiment of straight-backed chairs, along with a heavily carved sideboard, spilling over with the necessary assembly of silver, crystal, and china.

In discussing the objects that filled these essential public rooms, as well as bedrooms, sitting rooms, and assorted specific spaces of the articulated Victorian home (where there was a room for every possible purpose—music rooms, sitting rooms, libraries, sewing rooms), I refer except where noted, to the culture and attitudes of the country's emerging middle and upper-middle classes. These were the groups who, in their passion for the home, made Currier & Ives' classic *American Homestead* series (1868–1869) one of the company's most widely circulated sets—partly because of its seasonal portrayal of the ideal home, in an unquestionably idyllic setting, but perhaps, too, for its use of the then-magic words *American* and *home*. It was these home-conscious, object-conscious Victorians, then, who bequeathed us the greatest number of objects and artifacts for study and whose values of domesticity and solid home life created and ruled 19th-century America's popular taste.

3

HE VICTORIANS AND THEIR COLLECTING

That collectors today have such a bounty of Victoriana to choose from stems from the fact that Victorians were themselves the first great American collectors, happy inhabitants of an era that celebrated *things*. With great rooms and small filled with puffy, upholstered furniture, brass

sconces and chandeliers, overmantels heavy with shelves, shelves burdened with bric-a-brac, it was indeed an acquisitive age. In the homes of the well-to-do, one would also find a few carefully selected objects of foreign origin—Japanese screens, Dutch clocks, Moorish and Egyptian accents, tapestries from Venice, and more. These were important additions—purse-proud testimony of a family's ability to travel abroad, of their purported culture and sophistication in being able to appreciate such items. Here and there, one would also find examples of handmade fancywork (so necessary, it was felt, for the warm, cozy "home" feeling the Victorians valued above all). These might be beaded wall pockets, laboriously worked embroidered bookmarks and screens, handsome needlework cushions, hand-stitched mottos, perhaps even a decorated foot muff.

And finally, just to keep the whole from becoming too feminine—too affected—homeowners would add a dash of the unexpected—objects celebrating the fruits of nature and the glory of the environment: pinecone wall brackets, feather and moss work, "rustic" frames assembled from gnarled bits of seasoned wood. "We have been into rooms which, by simple disposition of articles of this kind, have been made to have an air so poetic and attractive, that they seemed more like a nymph's cave than any thing in the real world," effused Miss Beecher and Mrs. Stowe, in their popular and otherwise prosaic guide *The American Woman's Home* (1869).

How the Victorians loved things!

The occupation of plain sewing, with implements like these, *above,* filled the days of Victorian women. For paying a call or sitting in front of the evening fire with one's spouse, however, a woman presented a more captivating sight if she busied her hands with a bit of fancywork, *opposite.*

The prospect of new parlor carpet had one New York family fairly quivering with excitement in the 1860s, as they eagerly anticipated how well it would set off their "few good bits of bronze, a clock, the figure of Minerva with shield and spear balanced by side ornaments of classic urns." The old carpet had visually "outraged" the good pictures that hung in the parlor rooms, but a new one, well. . . . Hasten the day for the choosing! In sumptuous Oriental tones and in a durable Brussels weave, it would be just right.

The worldly Mark Twain was said to be so enamored of the fancy carving on the costly bed he bought in 1878 that he and his wife habitually slept in it backward—for a better view of the intricately carved headboard. Fascinated with the era's inventions (and indulging a bit himself by patenting a self-pasting scrapbook and a new kind of vest buckle), Twain, a most acquisitive Victorian and the quintessential Yankee, was also among the first to buy a fountain pen, a typewriter, a phonograph, and a telephone (the latter apparently dissatisfying him for some time). He nearly ruined himself in making his home the showplace of the neighborhood and worthy of his adored wife, Livy.

The Victorian love of domesticity and acquisition thrived even on the American frontier, where rags were turned into rugs, old dresses into curtains, and the arrival of a handsome pressed-glass bread plate inscribed "Give Us This Day Our Daily Bread" (one of the most popular items from those new mail-order houses) was an eagerly awaited event.

Victorians, while not the first to

Women's magazines consistently presented subtle forms of indoctrination into the cult of rustic adornment. *Opposite,* for example, this fashion plate from *Harper's Bazar* (ca. 1882) celebrates the glories of nature. Instructional pages in magazines offered how-tos for an almost alarming number of handcrafted "natural" objects, from handicraft trays, *above,* inlaid with wheat and grasses, to rugged antler-crowned timepieces, *right.*

collect, were the first to do so at all levels of society. Before the 1830s and 1840s, collecting had been the province of the wealthy alone. With the advent of industrialization—and low-cost machine-made goods—collecting could now be enjoyed by all and sundry. For those who couldn't afford fine cut glass, for example, pressed glass offered not just an inexpensive alternative, but one with a beauty of its own. Available from about the 1850s onward, pressed glass could be had in hundreds of patterns and shapes. In lieu of costly sterling, Victorians had silverplate, which could fill any sideboard with dramatic, glittering wares, at about half the price. J. C. Loudon was one tastemaker who, as early as 1839, urged everyone, even the most modest cottage dweller, to collect. Curious stones, minerals, and ores, he said, filled a worthy place on the humble country whatnot. Further, just as industrialization brought about a far-ranging prosperity—a new, upwardly mobile middle class with plenty of means, eager to acquire—Victorian invention yielded many more objects than a collector could ever have dreamed of—cut-glass toothpick holders, butter dishes and revolving caster sets, match safes, mustard jars, and little silverplate baskets to hold sweets or flowers. There were dozens of different kinds of spoons. For the first time, everything—from penny teapot to sterling porringer, from Currier & Ives print to Old Master—was available to all.

The Victorians were introduced to some of these items at the great world's fairs and exhibitions the era was famous

Mail order boomed in the 1870s, 1880s and 1890s, as major catalogue operations purveyed objects of all kinds across America. Even families homesteading in the most remote settlements found that life in a crude sod house or dugout could be made bearable with such luxuries as a stove, pots, and mixing bowls, *below,* as well as lamps, clocks, or even a piano, delivered right to one's door.

for. With improved means of travel, people were able to attend these events in greater numbers than ever before. These included the Crystal Palace Exposition in New York (1853), the Philadelphia Centennial (1876), and the 1893 World's Columbia Exposition in Chicago. Victorians were also introduced to goods in mail-order catalogues and magazines. If they lived near or visited a city, they could shop in a new and fascinating kind of emporium, the "department" store, which was exactly what its name implied. Whatever the source, the rising and ambitious middle classes were now able to cram their homes with an abundance of wonderful, factory-produced furnishings and objects (and at relatively low prices).

Often, Victorian manufacturers faced with overproduction sold their surplus to itinerant peddlers who brought these goods to out-of-the-way areas. There, these items, far more highly regarded than what was handmade, were warmly and eagerly received. Linens, generally believed by Victorian housewives to be overpriced in the run-of-the-mill general stores of the day, were popular, as were tin kitchen items, small gadgets, and notions like nutmeg graters and mechanical sweepers. The success of these enterprising early traveling salesmen probably explains why so many of these Victorian household curiosities turn up in rural America today.

The torrent of furnishings that flowed forth as a result of the country's booming productivity and sudden wealth, however, brought with it a critical predicament of taste. Newly affluent people were simply unprepared for the vast selection suddenly put before them. Which set of china should they buy? How and where should they display it? Which knickknacks, furnishings, and carpets, were fashionable—and "right"? Home, after all, was meant to be a glorious haven of beauty and charm—that's what society decreed, and even the learned clergy concurred. According to Reverend W. K. Tweedie in *Home, a Book for the Family Circle* (1874), the mission in furnishing a home was to create "a paradise of peace and purity," an "Eden," with much—nay, all—depending on home influence and care. Addie E. Heron, the prolific editor of *Home Art, a Journal Devoted to Interior Decoration,* added to the anxiety by including a talent for home decor among the prerequisites of a good wife. "It is certainly the first duty of a wife and mother to make home the pleasantest and happiest spot on earth," she wrote.

In the face of such widely held views, furnishing the home/sanctuary became a daunting task. In the cities, a clerk able to advise credibly on which fabric or drapery was tasteful, up-to-date, and genteel became the bewildered lady's savior. Out west, newcomers were pumped for information on current trends of the fashionable world, even if it had been some time since they'd left that world behind. The experience of one mid-century Oregon pioneer was common. "Although I had now been absent from civilization—otherwise Ohio—for more than a year, I was still considered an authority on the

Victorian women, relentless in their industry, filled their homes with all sorts of fancy-work—sentimental needlework pictures and elaborate shell art creations in shadow boxes (examples of which are shown *above*).

matter of dress and fashion," she wrote.

To the rescue came an army of self-appointed tastemakers, holding forth from the platforms of the magazines, books, and women's journals of the day. In some of the more remote frontier towns, the fortunate owner of a "lady's book" (even an issue more than a year old) was frequently consulted on matters of fashion, home furnishings, etiquette, needlework motifs, and table settings. A few grease spots on the pages of these now vintage magazines testify to their frequent use. Women used homemade oiled tracing paper to copy and exchange the patterns and designs published in magazines. And throughout the century, a proliferation of household guidebooks directed crucial domestic decisions.

The home journals, in particular, expounded on the multitudes of handworked elegancies with which women could and should beautify their homes, rather than be faced with unsightly, unadorned bareness. "Women should develop her artistic nature and give herself full scope in home adornment," explained May Perrin Goff in *The Household* (1881). The items created were important symbols of domesticity and feminine nature. Lack of them in a home certainly called a woman's character into question.

The skills necessary to create much of the handiwork (embroidery, crocheting, netting, knitting, lace work, painted theorems, and many others) were known as "accomplishments." Facility at needlework, the ability to draw or paint, to sing, play a musical instrument, speak French, were the talents "accomplished"

Even when she went visiting, a lady's workbag—a dressy one, that is, *left*—and, most likely, a pretty pair of scissors, *bottom left*—usually went along. The possession of a smattering of fashionable accomplishments, a modest facility in artistic pursuits, as *below,* as well as the ability to do fashionable needlework, *bottom,* enhanced a woman's value and appeal to suitors. The exquisite beadwork slippers, *opposite,* probably were a gift for a fortunate and favored gentleman.

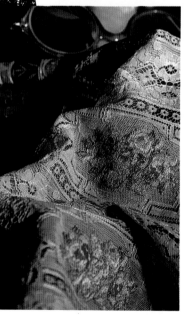

young women were praised for and that made them marriageable. China painting, the amateur painting of "blanks" (undecorated pieces of china) made expressly for this purpose, was probably the most fashionable and ladylike accomplishment of the 1890s. China-painting clubs, societies, and classes existed all over the country; instruction and patterns were even available by correspondence course! Caroline Harrison, wife of President Benjamin Harrison (1889–1992), was a devotee of the art, liberally adorning White House candlesticks, cracker boxes, and milk pitchers with her hand-painted specimens of flowers, fruit, and bucolic shepherdesses. Mrs. Harrison was especially partial to recording her favorite flower, the orchid, and was said to have painted orchids on dozens of dishes, for souvenir-hungry White House visitors.

Needlework—especially fancywork—though if not quite as stylish, was probably the most popular skill a lady interested in handiwork could acquire. Indeed, a woman could hardly escape that interest without exposing herself to moral criticism. "Decorative effort of some kind is a necessary part of home culture," one book admonished homemakers. "Do not let your children grow up amid uncouth and unlovely surroundings."

Indoctrination into the cult of needlewomen began early, and young girls' diaries contain endless mentions of interminable needlework projects. "I ought to buy me a new thimble and some scissors for I carried my sewing to school to-day . . . very carelessly and [it] dropped out and got lost," wrote an eleven-year-

SESAME AND LILIES
by
JOHN RUSKIN

old in 1854. A few months later, she noted: "I am sewing a sheet over and over for Grandmother and she puts a pin in to show me my stint before I can go out to play. I am always glad when I get to it." And: "I am also knitting on some wooden needles. . . . Grandmother has raveled it out several times because I dropped stitches. It is rather tedious."

No doubt it was. But schooled the right way, by the time she reached young ladyhood, in addition to the plain sewing of sheets and linens, a girl would have been adept at embroidery, beadwork, petit point and needlepoint, working on footstools, slippers, fans, handy little wall pockets, eyeglass cases, or even a pair of gentleman's suspenders. "It was so awfully good of you to work all these things, for me," says young Dick Mayne, an eligible bachelor in a sentimental novel of the period. The young lady of his fancy had "embroidered a most exquisite mantel-piece valence, and Phillis and Dulce [her sisters] had worked the corners of a green cloth with wonderful daffodils and bulrushes to cover Dick's shabby table; and Dick's soul had been filled with ravishment at the sight of these gifts." Such gifts were appreciated and highly regarded. "Fancy," he thought, "putting in all those stitches for me."

After mid-century, fancywork reigned. Hand-crocheted antimacassars (later called tidies)—the doilies placed on chairs to prevent Macassar oil, a popular men's hair dressing, from staining the upholstery—were everywhere. Homes simply overflowed with objects of genteel domesticity—fancy dresser, bureau, and

Musical ability—to be able to sing or play an instrument—was esteemed, and young women were often called upon to perform or "exhibit" their talents at social gatherings, as portrayed in this engraving (ca. 1874).

commode scarves; five o'clock tea cloths; hairpin holders; and a thousand and one dainty trifles. "In the appointments of a house, there is at present a mania for adornment," admitted one household guide, as all women, regardless of income, were pressed to try their hands at fancywork. "Now do not say you cannot afford it; you can afford it because it is one of the necessities and not a luxury of life," insisted Addie Heron, in her *Fancy Work for Pleasure or Profit* (1894).

With objects so fraught with meaning and social significance, it is hardly surprising that the Victorians turned to the sage advice of Clarence Cook and Charles Lock Eastlake, Harriet Prescott Spofford, Maria Parloa (whose column, sweepingly titled "Everything about the House except Cooking," was widely read), the aforementioned Beecher sisters (Catherine E. Beecher and Harriet Beecher Stowe), and many others to help them along the way. It was said that in the 1870s, there wasn't a newlywed couple in America who went furniture shopping without Eastlake's best-selling *Hints on Household Taste* in hand. In 1882, with aestheticism and the fad of "art for art's sake" overtaking American homes, 28-year-old Oscar Wilde (admitting to 26) took his widely publicized American lecture tour. Speaking on "The House Beautiful," "The English Renaissance," and "The Interior and Exterior Decoration of Houses" to audiences of record size, he advised on the smallest home detail. Wilde had an opinion on everything. He specified how high to hang hallway pictures. He outright condemned wall-to-wall floor coverings (dust-collecting and unhealthy), along with the Victorians' beloved stuffed birds on the mantel. He firmly preferred brass door knockers to bells, and he lauded the eternal beauties of yellow silk (yellow being a favorite shade of the aesthetes).

Despite sometimes conflicting advice on collecting and furnishing from Wilde and his fellow tastemakers, most Victorians were hardly avid antiquarians, hoarding objects from the historic past. Far from it. For the most part, this passion for the past came only in future generations (although the Philadelphia Centennial Exhibition of 1876 did spur an interest in America's colonial heritage). Even so, only a few Victorians recognized value in American antiques of past centuries. A family might sit on fine, old, black-painted Hitchcock chairs with square seats and delicate gold tracings and sip tea from eggshell cups with tiny, raised lavender flowers, without ever suspecting the worth of these "old family things."

Instead, for the most part, typical Victorians collected products from their own century. At first, this collecting was somewhat restrained; early Victorian homes tended to retain the sparseness of the previous decades, perhaps with a few objects from previous generations, i.e., a handcrafted chair, a pair of silver candlesticks brought from the East. Along with classical Empire and Gothic Revival furniture and boldly patterned carpeted floors, a parlor might contain a lamp and a pair of vases, and, except for a portrait or two, a landscape and perhaps an old-

Nearly every mantel held a clock like the one *below,* **in a carved oak case.**

fashioned silhouette hung on a ribbon, the walls were rather bare. Lithographs of historical scenes or sentimental allegories and maps were other austere accessories. A clock would have been something of a prized possession (time was told by the farmer's workday, sunup to sundown, a tradition that industrialization and factories, literally run "by the clock," ultimately changed). Always placed on the mantel, it would have been flanked by candlesticks, bronzes, and a bust or two.

Yet things were changing. The silver collection had already moved from the occasional and discreet heirloom tea set on a cart in the parlor corner to a far more showy display—frequently pieces ornamented in bold relief—in the dining room. Gold-banded dinnerware was fairly inexpensive and popular; mirrors—"looking glasses"—bell jars, and brackets for vases were becoming fashionable. A room might sport a thermometer or barometer. By the 1850s, spurred by industrialization and the proliferation of railroads that made rapid transportation of goods possible, items once considered accessories had become necessities.

The Victorians' collecting can be broken down into several specific themes. First and foremost, they collected objects with a certain fulsome opulence, objects that clearly spoke of material wealth and success. This meant acquiring objects that were not only expensive but—just as important—were *expensive looking.* During the mid-Victorian period, mahogany and rosewood furniture with rich, bright upholstery and lots of creamy-

Ornamentation, particularly gilding, as seen on these late 19th-century porcelains, *above and left,* was often a measure of an object's desirability. In addition to fostering a sense of richness, gilding also reflected light, a highly regarded quality. *Opposite:* Parlor carpets—such as this elegant design, exhibited in the Crystal Palace in London during the Great Exhibition of 1851—were precious symbols of status and prosperity to upwardly striving Victorians.

white marble-topped tables fell into this category. This new Rococo Revival furniture, both fashionable and costly, made quite a sensation, appealing to those established in society as well as to those who aspired to social standing. The furniture's rollicking curves and (in the hands of master craftsmen like John Henry Belter, Joseph Meeks, or Alexander Roux) lavish and intricate carving not only proclaimed status but also held definite and appealing references to the wonders of nature by way of its sinuous carved fruit, grapes, vines, and flowers. When furnishing a parlor, a collection of Rococo Revival furniture, along with the accent of something imported (for instance, a chair in papier-mâché, a medium admired for its delicate femininity and the exotic qualities of its mother-of-pearl designs), provided quite a sophisticated look.

Often, the degree of adornment on the more costly collectibles was the measure of an item's desirability, whether ornate painting on a china plate, double rows of braided fringe on damask draperies, or lavish gilding—rich-looking and elegant, reflecting flashes of light everywhere. "Gilding is especially desirable if the room be on the dark side, for it supplies a light of its own, independent of sunlight," explained one 19th-century source book. The creation of light, of course, was a precious thing. And gilding there was—from gilded threads running through textiles to gilding on wallpapers, porcelains, and furniture.

In the 1870s and 1880s, flamboyant Renaissance Revival furniture became especially emblematic of good fortune. With its opulent ornamentation, sense of grandeur, and frequently massive size, it seemed an apt visual expression of the material bounty of the time. In order to afford such grand pieces—tall, profusely ornamented with gilding—one must have been doing well.

Victorian ornamentation didn't stop with china painting or carved furniture. Such elegancies, after all, might be expected. Adorned, any object could move from the plane of the basic to that of the luxurious. As a mark of material plenty and refinement, combined with a Victorian distaste for bareness, ornamentation blossomed on every imaginable surface, no matter how insignificant—doorknobs, hinges, parlor stoves, plumbing pipes. Even the tiny brass triangles tucked into stair corners to prevent the accumulation of dust and dirt were adorned with etched designs—and considered a particularly civilized and fastidious touch. Ornaments were carefully chosen for their appropriateness. Homemakers of the 1880s fittingly adorned walnut picture frames with pasted-on sliced walnuts.

Pictorial images and patterns provided yet another kind of ornamentation for the home and its objects. No better example exists than Victorian wall coverings, suddenly affordable to significant numbers of people in wonderful vibrant colors and exciting patterns. It is hard to fathom the visual impact these wallpapers had more than one hundred years ago when today our eyes are surfeited with images on everything from cereal boxes to sheets, shampoo, and

billboards. The 19th century was a world of black-and-white woodcuts and grainy newsprint likenesses. To own a book with illustrations was a special thing. To the average early Victorian, whose bedcovers and pillowcases, books and walls were almost uncompromisingly plain, the affordability of printed images on wall coverings and fabrics as well as on teacups and lampshades, trade cards and calendars, was a miraculous thing, bringing color and life to the contours of a room.

Parlor carpets, while commonplace today, were also key symbols of prosperity to upwardly striving Victorians. Before 1840, women were frequently obliged to make their own floor coverings, no inconsiderable task. As a family gained in means, handwoven coverings and old-fashioned rag carpets were scorned in favor of store-bought carpets as status symbols. "The soul of the apartment is the carpet," wrote none other than Edgar Allan Poe in an essay in *Gentleman's Magazine* (1840). "A judge at common law may be an ordinary man; a good judge of a carpet *must be* [italics his] a genius." So precious were carpets considered in the early Victorian years that one frontier woman purportedly hesitated to call on a neighbor because she had heard that the neighbor owned a Brussels carpet. As the story goes, the neighbor did own one, though no one ever saw it. The carpet was so highly regarded that it was never unrolled, lest it be spoilt.

Porcelains were also expressive of 19th-century wealth. They came in shapes and design motifs that, like the flatware

China, particularly featuring Aesthetically influenced designs, *above and opposite,* signaled not only material wealth, but also a familiarity with and appreciation of artistic good taste.

of the period, tended to follow contemporary furniture styles (during the 1850s, for example, china patterns with strong Rococo floral themes were popular; the Japanesque craze of the 1870s produced silver with bamboo handles), China platters, decorated boxes, and painted figurines would be elegantly arranged on mantels or cover the shelves of cabinets, whatnots, cupboards, and curio cases. The possession of fine old china instantly identified the three young sisters in Rosa N. Carey's *Not Like Other Girls* as "ladies," though now—plucky in the face of calamity—forced to try to earn their living as dressmakers: " 'They have so many nice things—pictures and old china and handsomely bound books, and all arranged so tastefully [described the sister of the village parson]. And before we went away, the old servant—she seems really quite a superior person—brought in an elegant little tea tray—the cups and saucers were handsomer even than yours, Miss Middleton—dark purple and gold. Just what I admire so—' 'Ah, reduced in circumstances! I told you so, Elizabeth,' ejaculated the colonel."

The old china, of course, was the clue to past glories. Even their workroom was "perfectly lovely with pictures and old china." Readers would have also immediately recognized elder sister Nan's appreciation for the family's heirloom china as evidence of her refinement, breeding, and femininity. Poor Nan. Although the display of the cherished Sèvres cup and saucer was necessary—"for people to see and be struck with their taste"—"the china was very dear to her. She did not care for

Victorian Americans avidly collected porcelains and china of all kinds, elaborately patterned in a form of china painting called potichimanie, *left,* or with simpler transfer-printed designs, *below.*

strangers to look at them and appraise their value. They were home treasures— sacred relics of the past."

For much of the era, alabaster vases were prized—a mantel pair would have been much admired. Alabaster's translucent, waxy whiteness (not to mention the evocative and musical sound of the word itself) aroused the Victorians' romantic instincts. That alabaster vases were imported added to their cachet. The same principle lay behind the exotic appeal of a bust or figurine carved in Carrara marble; owning such an item was notable. Things that were foreign were difficult to acquire and therefore highly esteemed.

In the 1870s, the fad for blue-and-white china took hold, and Victorians briskly collected blue-and-white during the rest of the century. As collectibles, though, these pieces offered a different kind of status. While the accumulation of china in general was a mark of material means, blue-and-white was also a recognizable symbol of the Aesthetic Movement, the widely publicized trend devoted to refined taste, arts, and culture. While an undergraduate at Oxford, Oscar Wilde proudly displayed two large blue china vases (possibly Sèvres) on his mantel, soon becoming famous for his facetious, "I find it harder and harder every day to live up to my blue china" (a remark quoted in *Punch* and satirized in a George du Maurier drawing). Wilde apparently went on to collect china with an abandon beyond his student means; he was later dunned for his extravagant, if aesthetically correct, purchases.

This page, clockwise from top: Victorian china, collected, displayed, and in use today. With gilding and Japanesque scenic designs; traditional blue-and-white on a Victorian overmantel; elegant Aesthetic dishes set on a modern glass table, and in close-up; an Aesthetic serving dish (and, partially visible nearby, an Aesthetic brass mirror); and richly ornamented and colored sunflower vases that reflect the artistic bent of the 1870s and 1880s.

By displaying Aesthetic Movement china and other approved objects liberally throughout their homes, followers of the philosophy (or those who pretended to be) suggested at least a nodding acquaintance with the arts and taste of the Orient. The Victorians liked to collect all sorts of china, but they had a special fondness for three particular types: majolica (for its appealing bold shapes, its richly shaded glazing, and the charm of those brilliant and gaudy colors); paper-thin translucent Beleek, with its characteristic delicate crimped edges; and Parian ware, an unglazed porcelain the Victorians hoped looked just like marble that could be used for statuary. (The very name *Parian,* a nod to the Greek island of Paros, where the marble for ancient statuary was quarried, reflects the antiquarian interests of Victorians.)

A flashy display of silver on the dining-room sideboard was also typical, immediately suggesting both elegance and substantial means. The same went for cut glass, which was free blown or mold shaped, then cut into elaborate, faceted patterns. As late as 1901, a short story, "The Newport Luncheon" in *The Ladies World,* has snobbish "half-bored" Platt Kingston, the local arbiter of taste, advising young Winifred Elmslie, a Chicago wife, on the parties that would propel her into the upper reaches of Newport society: "Have always lots of the choicest flowers and champagne in lavish quantities of the rarest brands," he advised. "Even at your 'afternoons' have champagne in pitchers—in pitchers, mind, of the most expensive glass."

A collector's rare cache of Victorian silver, *opposite,* with Aesthetic ornamentation. During the second half of the century, travel became an important ritual of fashionable life. As more people found the means and the courage to journey, souvenirs such as silver and silverplated teaspoons, *above,* became popular keepsakes. Victorian pressed glass, *below and overleaf,* provided an attractive alternative to those who could not afford cut glass.

Silver and crystal, traditional and precious signs of Victorian status, soon gave way to lesser versions—19th-century silverplate and pressed glass, which enabled almost anyone to assemble an abundant and impressive display. The designs of 19th-century silverplate tended to represent a whimsical and inventive point of view, lighter, more experimental compared to sedate sterling. A five- or seven-piece silverplate tea set became the most desired wedding gift for the middle-class Victorian bride, who also coveted silverplate tureens, butter dishes, berry bowls, fruit stands, and other holloware. Small novelties like napkin rings, knife rests, and menu holders were also enthusiastically collected. The quirkiness and idiosyncrasies of their designs (with nursery characters, monkeys, owls, and other eccentricities) are revealing commentaries on the outlandish extremes of late 19th-century taste.

The production of Victorian pressed glass, which first came into use during the 1820s and 1830s (previously tableware had been blown or shaped in a mold), reached a peak as the century progressed, evolving from rather heavy, early designs (in thick, bulky glassware) and simple, ribbed patterns to historically inspired motifs (the Lincoln Drape in imitation of the mourning banners that festooned buildings and windows following the assassination) and delicate lacy patterns. Machine-pressing techniques allowed for the manufacture of pressed-glass pieces in thousands of patterns at very low cost. Early pressed glass was clear, but later the Victorians collected

glassware in a rich range of colors—amber, ruby, rose, cranberry, green, and amethyst.

In addition to objects that were obvious proclamations of material wealth, the Victorians were also taken with the new, the progressive, the up-to-date. In the last quarter of the century, for example, matching suites of furniture (an innovation of the 1850s, passé twenty years later) were spurned for a determinedly eclectic style, Mixing Renaissance Revival, Turkish, Egyptian, patent pieces, and even wicker—in a seemingly nonchalant way—brought a new and fashionable quality that appealed to the Victorian sense of style.

Turkish corners—wonderfully draped concoctions of fringe and fabric, sensual and exotic tapestries, pillows, scimitars, and brass—were also popular. They seemed so new, trendy, and chic. During the 1890s, a bewildered fifteen-year-old girl returned home to find that her mother had turned her top-floor bedroom into a Turkish delight. "My bed was a divan, broad and luxurious. Over it hung a canopy of rich Persian stuff of lively blues and greens. Draperies of the same material hung in thick folds at the side, looped up gracefully, but effectively kept out the air. . . . Little tables of wood and mother-of-pearl were placed at certain strategic points; each carried a delicate long-spouted copper coffee urn and diminutive cups. Dull brass lamps sprouted from the ceiling. It all had a really warm and seductive air, but was not particularly conducive to the mastery of algebra or Latin."

Objects disguised as something else, such as the charming pincushion, *below*, shaped like a lady's slipper and studded with hat pins, appealed to the Victorian sense of whimsy.

Despite these drawbacks—and the fact that neither she nor her friends could move around in the room without causing disaster—the Turkish corner had to stay. Popular taste dictated that every fashionable home have a Turkish parlor, and there was no other place for it in the house.

In their obsession with the new, Victorians filled their homes not only with the latest in furnishings, objects, and textiles (the craze for Japanese goods had them enthusiastically collecting paper fans, many of which you can still find today) but also indulged in the latest fads. "Colored" luncheons, as described in *The Ladies Home Journal* (August 1899), whereby all the courses were red, blue, or green, were one passing fancy. A menu for a red luncheon consisted of tomato soup, hot lobster, buttered beets, strawberry punch, and raspberry charlotte. A green one featured pea soup, fish with spinach sauce, potatoes with parsley, peas, mint punch, lettuce salad with green Japanese wafers, and charlotte covered with pistachio nuts. A few years later, in September 1901, another magazine, *The Ladies' World,* noted that "lemon parties have 'broken out' again." For these, the hostess sent out invitations on yellow paper, requested guests to bring a lemon with them, strung yellow lanterns and yellow garlands on her porch and lawn, wore a yellow gown and, of course, among other refreshments, served lemonade. "In arranging such an entertainment, one's ideas grow as the preparations progress and many quaint notions can be carried out."

Every fad, every new idea, every gadget had its following, from the newfangled ice-cream scoop in 1876—ice cream being a favored Victorian dessert —to Edison's phonograph. In the dining room, the desire for all things new meant a utensil for every possible purpose—fish forks, oyster ladles, berry dishes, sugar tongs, and revolving fruit-knife holders. We collect these today as charming oddities; the Victorians collected them partly because they were fascinated by their newness (and proud of their ability to afford them) but also because their appreciation of such very specialized tools was clear-cut evidence of their innate gentility and refinement.

Objects disguised as other objects were yet another category that tickled the Victorian fancy. How cunning and playful to own a pincushion shaped like a swan or a heart, or a papier-mâché slipper that concealed a candy box. Such trinkets were all thought remarkably clever and were displayed by the Victorians with particular pride.

At first, the camera was a symbol of the progressive life, captivating Victorians who were now able to see for the first time accurate likenesses of presidents and politicians, famous authors, popular stars of the theater and music halls, great beauties, and even the royal families of Europe (the latter, no doubt, proved something of a disappointment). Three-dimensional photo cards with clever stories and cunning scenes and the stereoscopes used to view them became standard parlor accessories: with them one could experience Niagara Falls, the

The Victorians adored colorful trade cards, *top,* which were produced by manufacturers and merchants from the 1870s through the 1890s to promote their goods and services. As it does today, 19th-century travel provided the opportunity to take family photographs, *above left,* as proof of the trip.

Always intrigued by innovation, the Victorians eagerly collected the three-dimensional photo cards, *above right.* A simple stereoscope cost about 25 cents in the 1860s and early 1870s, costly in a time when a laborer made between $2 and $4 a week.

San Francisco fire, and scenes of foreign lands without ever leaving the parlor settee.

Very quickly, though, photography became an instrument of sentiment. As professional photo studios cropped up in all the big cities (and particularly in seaside resorts and other vacation spots), every family wanted pictures of themselves to take home and display as cherished family mementos. First there were daguerreotypes, then tintypes—both perfect for collecting—encased in elegant leather or gilt holders lined with velvet or plush. These early pictures littered the tabletops, mantels, and shelves of Victorian homes.

Massive photo albums, perhaps the most sentimental accessory of all, soon found their way into almost every 19th-century home, their status as a particularly cherished keepsake evidenced by their impressive appearance—padded, covered in plush, velvet, or celluloid and often handsomely bound with a heavy metal clasp. Albums usually sat in a place of honor on the parlor table and provided many happy hours of entertainment for family members and visitors.

The Victorians' insatiable appetite for sentiment led them to collect other types of albums, too. In these, ladies assembled all sorts of romantic keepsakes —dried flowers and pressed bouquets; snippets of poetry; pen and ink drawings of leaves, trees, children, or animals; copies of famous paintings; charming chromolithographed scraps; decorative cards; romantic sayings; quotations; and souvenirs of trips and playbills. An artistically

Photos such as these, *top,* filled tabletops, mantels, and shelves. Unframed "cabinet cards" (so-called because they were often displayed on top of cabinets), could be stored in the family Bible or preserved in heavy photo albums (*above,* two albums and, in the foreground, a collar box). Collections of engravings, maps, and architectural or botanical prints provided great pleasure to the Victorians. Studying them was even considered a respectable pastime for courting couples, *below.*

arranged album was a creation of pride to the young lady who owned it, to be handed around and admired. Favored gentlemen might even be persuaded to sketch a cartoon, pen a few lines of poetry, or provide some other artistic contribution. When completed (which was seldom), these collections were regarded as definitive works of art.

Autograph albums were another kind of keepsake. During the 1870s and 1880s, these new, expensive items were all the rage among young people; school chums wrote what were rightly called sentiments in each other's treasured books, with the beautiful penmanship ("a copper-plate hand") so prized at the time. Calling cards (also called name cards) bordered with hearts, birds, and flowers were collected and pasted in albums as well. Holiday and birthday cards and cheerful "Greetings," squirreled away by the sentimental, acquisitive Victorians, are apt illustrations of the degree to which the 19th century relished ornament. Even these were embellished with silk fringe, tassels, and metallic gilding. And there were album quilts, another sentimental gift, with each block worked and signed by a different contributor.

Embroidered mottos like Home, Sweet Home, and other domestic pieties —which Victorians collected to proclaim their hospitality from doorframes and stair wells, were also expressions of sentiment. Today, one can still find them, often in their original rustic twig or pinecone frames, which, it was felt, gave a bit of individuality to their look.

Many Victorians, insecure about

their johnny-come-lately social status, sought out mementos they felt would imply background and family ancestry. In addition to placing cupboards of old china (inherited or assumed to be so) in the parlor, a fine set of portraits hung in the entryway would also impress visitors with a family's distinguished background and connections. Alternatively, portraits might hang in the dining room, another traditional place for a family gallery. A grandfather clock, also in the entry, served a similar purpose. Its pride of place suggested that it had been passed down through the generations; if newly purchased, it stood as a sign of family wealth. Hallway clocks served a practical function, too, in those days when not everyone owned a watch.

Another object collected as an icon of family background was the ancestral chest, "the more antique, the better," according to one popular household guide. Its value, of course, was not its antiquity (one that merely looked old would have done just as well), but what its presence implied. "With its brass or bronze handles, its carved woodwork, it looks as if it might have come over in the *Mayflower* and held the riches of the whole family. Those who have them not [sic] are having the designs copied and imitated in rich woods and a goodly amount of money they cost, too." During the 1880s, many of these old chests, which had previously been used to hold carpenter's tools or were tucked away in the attics, were reclaimed and returned to places of honor in the forefront of the home. Above them, on the wall or in the

Racks and folio stands, *above,* which might have held one's collection of exotic animal or botanical prints or views of foreign lands and demonstrated one's cultural leanings, were a common parlor convention. Screens too, particularly ones with Japanese-style designs such as the one *below,* would have been on display in the parlor of the 1870s or 1880s.

corner of the corridor, old armor, heraldic plaques, and other antiquities would have completed the picture.

Closely related to objects emphasizing family background and breeding (real or imagined) were those things Victorians gathered around themselves as indications of their learning, culture, and familiarity with the arts. Musical instruments, a piano, or harp were considered necessary additions to a parlor, or housed in a separate music room. A harp, in particular, was regarded almost as an advertisement of grace, wealth, and refinement, and a young Victorian lady was thought to make a pleasing picture delicately fingering its strings. Paintings, steel engravings, watercolors, lithographs, chromos and other prints, sculptures, busts, figurines—any semblance of fine art—also served the purpose. A. J. Downing wrote that "nothing gives an air of greater refinement than good prints or engravings hung [on the] parlor walls," advising that one steer clear of "trashy colored showy prints" of the ordinary kind and choose engravings or lithographs that were copies of old or modern masters.

Lithographs were the most popular form of art in the average Victorian home, followed by very proper wood and steel engravings. Of course, many Victorians, new to the ownership of works of art, often had to be reminded how and where to display such things. The proper height to hang a picture, for instance, depended on its medium—whether watercolor, engraving, or oil painting—as well as the room in which it was dis-

played. Similar strictures ruled the display of sculpture. It was not to be placed in a window facing the street, as one expert admonished (where apparently many proud Victorians placed objects of statuary) "so all could see they possessed them," never minding that the return they received was a usually uninspiring rear view. Instead, a sculpture should be bathed in "mellow light, where shadows can play on it, hiding and softening its outlines."

A painting casually resting on an easel in the parlor denoted an appreciation of fine art: that it was not hung was considered an appropriately offhand touch. An unframed painting was even better since it gave the impression that the owner "dabbled." Paintings propped against the wall had a similar effect.

Portfolios of sketches, engravings, and prints of exotic animals and botanical specimens demonstrated one's lofty cultural leanings. Studying these prints together was a respectable pastime for a shy courting couple. Every month magazines offered new steel engravings, which could be cut out and added to one's collection.

Bronzes and marble busts (and for the less well-to-do, those in plaster or Parian) symbolized culture and familiarity with the classics; ancient and contemporary poets, composers, literary figures, mythological gods, statesmen, and soldiers were all honored. Once again, particularly during the 1870s and 1880s, anything Japanese or even purporting to reflect that taste indicated artistic sensibilities. Japanese screens, objects

Because of improved transportation, the Philadelphia Centennial of 1876 was more widely attended and consequently had greater influence than earlier expositions, further igniting interest in collecting objects of Japanese and Turkish origin, such as the faux bamboo furnishings and Aesthetic curios in this collector's home, *opposite.* A collection of Parian sculpture, *below,* and the offhand touch of draped artwork, *bottom,* casually resting on an easel denoted an appreciation of fine art to social climbers, who longed to possess not only material goods but culture.

adorned with peacock or sunflower motifs, delicate paper fans, and bamboo stands fell into this category. So clear was their message, that even displayed in an otherwise typically Victorian upholstered room, the philosophical ground they were meant to cover was unquestionably apparent. In the same vein, a decorative tile mounted on a stand and placed on the mantel would be much admired by art-conscious Victorians for the subtle beauty of its design.

Despite their ardent need to be recognized as connoisseurs of the arts, 19th-century Americans were rather sanguine about copies of great art. They had no qualms about displaying them in their homes. Why not, they felt, show an appreciation for the finest? The distinction between an original and its reproduction seemed to escape them: Downing, one of the most respected tastemakers of the time, approved it as did others. "For the artistic touches one needs, choose carefully and judiciously," agreed Goff in *The Household.* "Upon the walls a few pictures; if you like heads of saints, choose old masters; if atmospheric effects with glories of gold and crimson sunsets, Turner; if cattle, where the dapple cows lie chewing their cud in content . . . in meadow land, Rosa Bonheur; if of dogs, Landseer, and so on." Copies all, of course. Working as a copyist of great works was an established route for art students and struggling young artists, who while studying in Europe churned out countless copies to satisfy the undiscriminating tastes of art-loving tourists.

Books were also necessary symbols of culture, "as much a part of the home as pictures or furniture or carpets," according to Georgene Corry Benham in *Polite Life and Etiquette, What is Right and the Social Arts.* "A home without books is desolate indeed." A few finely bound books, displayed on a parlor chair or table, very nicely suggested both the owner's literacy (should that be in question) and a familiarity with great works. Some tastemakers objected to the practice on the grounds that it could give the impression that, heaven forbid, one didn't have a home library, very much a status symbol in the 1880s. "Do not be content to buy a few scattering books here and there, but have a bookcase and put in it, from time to time…varieties of books," dictated Benham, obviously on to the popular subterfuge. "Every home should have a library, if possible." Besides, book covers and bindings were wonderfully ornamental in and of themselves, rich with ornate lettering, fanciful gilded designs, and lavish and colorful frontispieces.

Certain refinements in what the Victorians collected had less to do with the world of higher art than with the etiquette and niceties of the day. The presence of curios in a wall cabinet or an étagère—relics, specimens, objects of art, even a book casually placed on a side table, its cover in full view—was a gambit designed to raise the level of conversation beyond the topics of fashion, dress, or scandal. (Even then, it seems, Americans were trying to escape the gossip mongers.) Chromos and lithographs with soothing pastoral themes were meant to create an atmosphere of gentility and re-

The ideal version of refined Victorian taste, as seen in Clarence Cook's popular book, *The House Beautiful* (1878), *top,* featured a requisite hanging wall cabinet and choice curios. Books, as evidence of literacy, *above,* were considered as much a part of the home as its furniture or carpets. As museums gained importance during the second half of the century, the home too became a "museum," *opposite,* filled with the strange and the exotic. One place for all these curios was the library.

finement and evoke the virtues of a tranquil home life.

While pastoral scenes might hang in the parlor and rosy-cheeked cherubs gambol on teacups and album covers, the Victorian world of collecting wasn't all sweetness and light. The library, for example, was a masculine preserve that was also a darkly fascinating stronghold of the eccentric and the bizarre, a veritable receptacle for all the curiosities of nature the Victorians avidly acquired. In the library—over and above the requisite books, maps, globes, and scientific instruments—one might find collections of fossils, bones, minerals, rocks, dried starfish, butterflies, moths, and, if fortunate, relics (archaeological discoveries of the time, particularly from Egypt and Rome, stirred the Victorian imagination). Not to be overlooked were expertly done specimens of taxidermy, a popular home pastime in which ladies indulged. Following an instructive beauty section on the care of the hands—"All admire pretty hands, and yet how few are the happy possessors of them"—one book blithely goes into a detailed, not to say grotesque, discussion of the stuffing and mounting of birds: "Mount the birds, if possible, in a manner to be suggestive of life. Let the wild duck or the fish-hawk be surrounded with reeds, rushes, aquatic sprays or willow twigs. Locate the velvety brown partridge over her nest of eggs, partly hidden among half-dry grasses. Plant the woodpecker defiantly upon a leafless bough. Do not give them a stiff awkward appearance, as if the wind had blown them, in their places and they had frozen

there, but arrange them as naturally as possible."

The Victorians' fascination with taxidermy stemmed from their affectionate wonder at nature's wildlife and a need to bring it into the home. In general, though, Victorians revered the curious, the exotic, the beautiful, and the strange in equal degree, appreciating the juxtaposition of odd textures and unusual scents. Fossils, odd rocks, mossy birds' nests, and such were educational, uplifting; they brought one into contact with the wonders of the world. Sometimes, too, these curiosities found their way into the parlor. A small table or shelf might have been a showcase for a pretty grouping of natural curiosities—a chunk of quartz, a cluster of pearly shells, a skeletonized leaf, a branch of petrified wood—to be carefully examined by guests while giving evidence of the host's sophisticated awareness of nature. Bell jars filled with artistic natural scenes, sometimes enhanced with shells or glass shavings, and groupings of birds and small creatures were a common parlor sight, representing the 19th century's first stirrings of interest in the world at large.

Coins, geodes, and shells; birds' eggs and nests; and bits of polished ivory and other specimens would fill the corners of the room. Small curio cabinets would house these collections, which were organized into "little museums," the easier to exhibit one's prized collection to curious onlookers. Or, they would occupy the library shelves, counterpoints to the dusty bound volumes, monographs, and folios.

Godey's Lady's Book **in March 1855 recommended the ornamental shade, trimmed with actual greenery,** *above.* **The world of nature was also explored through collections of stuffed birds and animals, preserved in natural settings under ubiquitous bell jars,** *below.*

Certain 19th-century handiwork also falls into the category of Victorian oddities. Hair art, for example, is very much a combination of Victorian sentiment, the handiwork tradition, and the bizarre. Intricately braided and twisted hairwork pictures, hair wreaths, hair jewelry, even hairwork geneological family trees were some of the sentimental tokens women painstakingly created from the hair of family and friends. The hair itself was saved by stuffing the combings from one's brush into a singular dresser-top accessory called a hair receiver, usually a delicately painted china container with a hole in its top, created expressly for that purpose.

Pressed seaweed specimens (seaweed fragments, dried and delicately pasted into different designs on sheets of board or paper) were another oddity that ladies loved to make. "An album of views of seaside resorts is very pretty when each picture is set in a frame of sea weeds," suggests one handbook, reminding enthusiasts that on each specimen, the name, date and locality should appear. The fragility of the seaweeds and mosses (called flowers of the sea) and the care with which they had to be handled made this an accomplishment few could master effectively.

Finally, the Victorians also had a weakness for souvenirs and commemoratives. The ability to travel was still new, and journeys of any kind were often fraught with hazards and dangers. In one Victorian novel, as the engine of the first steam-powered train started to roar, daring travelers faced the crowds of specta-

Shells and broken bits of porcelain were salvaged to make the quintessentially Victorian ornament, *above.* Intricately twisted and braided Victorian hair art, *far left and left,* was created as a memorial to the deceased or in honor of family ties and friendship.

tors, fairly puffed with importance. "The little ones whose fathers were in the train began to call good-bye and wave their hands and one old lady whose only son was going as one of the train assistants, began to sob aloud." Even the heroine felt the portentousness of the event, the honor of traveling so far to see "this great wonder of machinery." "She felt a little dubious about appearing on such a great occasion, almost in Albany, in a chintz dress and no wrap," we're told.

Journeys were anticipated with excitement and trepidation—even simple trips took as long as a week, and European tours stretched into months and sometimes years—and souvenirs were eagerly acquired as proof of worldliness

Victorians always brought back souvenirs from their travels, such as this Native American beadwork wallpocket, *opposite.* **Expositions also encouraged acquisition, and small fairs frequently sold inexpensive novelties and small glass and china ornaments (today collected as fairing) to visitors. Tiny glass and china slippers,** *above,* **were an unusually popular choice.**

and treasured mementos of where one had been.

Different kinds of souvenirs were collected at different times. Some items were simply fads, with little enduring significance. Small pressed-glass novelties such as toothpick holders, tiny umbrellas, wheelbarrows, cradles, animal shapes, and baskets, given away by glass companies at the booths at the Philadelphia Centennial, probably started the craze for the collecting of these inexpensive novelties. Other glass collectibles included tiny glass hats that advertised world's fairs, as well as glass shoes, boots, and slippers.

Seashells commemorated visits to the shore, something not everyone was able to do; the same went for painted

Similar to shellwork boxes, *top and above,* are heart-shaped or octagonal boxes known as sailors' valentines, gifts purchased and brought home by 19th-century sailors to their sweethearts. Because of their sentimental nature many were saved and can still be found today. Engravings also show similar Victorian shell pieces being peddled to tourists at the shore.

plates or dishes from such popular Victorian resorts as Newport or Saratoga. Souvenirs from the White House or, even more precious, keepsakes from a visit to Rome were symbols of the well traveled. In the classic *Little House* books by Laura Ingalls Wilder, a trip from De Smet, South Dakota, to Vinton, Iowa (neither a metropolis), was an event to be marked with souvenirs for the younger children. "Your Pa and I wanted our other girls to have something from Vinton, Iowa, where Mary is going to college," their mother explained.

For those Victorians fortunate enough to afford travel abroad, a vial of holy water, a shell, pebble or jar of sand, all to be proudly displayed in the parlor, were typical souvenirs. Other items included collectibles specifically printed to commemorate a historic event—Perry's opening of Japan, for example, sparked the craze for Oriental bric-a-brac. There were souvenirs honoring singer Jenny Lind's visit to America, and Lily Langtry's. The great world's fairs and expositions produced thousands of popular collectibles: paper banners, fans, flyers, and buttons, all noting the place and the date.

Collecting souvenir teaspoons was an important fad of the 1890s, and the Victorians loved assembling collections of sterling teaspoons, some engraved with dates, others with scenes or symbols of cities, hotels, or noted landmarks. Bowls, pitchers, or plates painted with scenes of well-known attractions like Niagara Falls or with representations of historic events were also popular collectibles.

Commemoratives, similar to souvenirs, came in the form of plates, cups, dishes, bowls, coins, and other items marking such occasions as royal coronations or presidential elections. All sorts of commemoratives, from cider mugs to creamware beakers, were created to honor Victoria's Silver (1887) and Diamond (1897) Jubilee years. Trophies and presentation silver, big, pompous pieces usually engraved with the name of the recipient and the date, were given as awards for service, as prizes (racing and yachting trophies were popular), and on the anniversaries of significant events.

With their possessions proclaiming materialism, heritage, sentiment, curiosity, and a concern for progress, education, culture, and the arts, the Victorians' attitude toward collecting—that more is more—was very much an expression of the climate and character of the times. While it was undoubtedly materialistic, Victorian collecting had an air of childlike joy far removed from the intrinsic meanness associated with the period. Unhampered by the guilt contemporary collectors sometimes claim they feel over active accumulation, the Victorians fully enjoyed their collections and doted on each new acquisition. A new print on the wall or another curio for the cabinet served as a potent and necessary reminder of what they had achieved; the acquisition of things nurtured the spirit. Along with obvious joy and naïve pride, a tender longing for security, a touching need for acceptance, permeated their multiclustered collections, making them all the more precious to collectors today.

To celebrate elections, coronations, and expositions, the Victorians produced hundreds of different types of commemoratives and souvenirs. *Top:* Pressed glass commemorative plates. *Above and right:* Popular souvenir spoons.

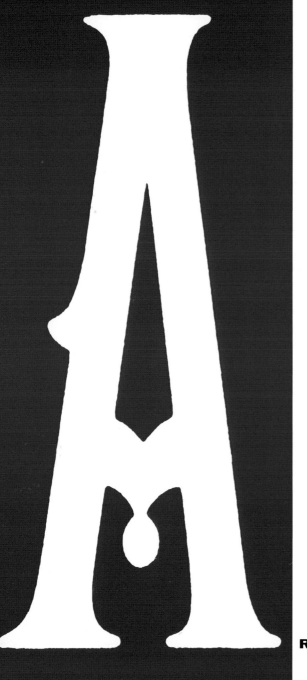

4

ARRANGEMENT AND **D**ISPLAY

The Victorians arranged and displayed their collectibles according to a set of strict guidelines. After all, this was a society governed by a code of behavior as narrow and unyielding as the stiff whalebone and canvas corsets in which women were obliged to confine their figures. What

you wore and how you wore it, how you ate and with whom you spoke, the way you sat in a chair or held a book, even permissible topics of conversation—all were rigorously prescribed.

Except for those with the most irreproachable ancestry, it must have been a harrowing time. Even the members of Mrs. Astor's favored Four Hundred surely must have shuddered every now and then as they narrowly missed committing some obscure faux pas. For example, the indelicacy of a man's leaving his hat and walking stick in the hallway instead of carrying them into the parlor could brand him as a boorish parvenu in the eyes of polite society. Emily Holt's *Encyclopedia of Etiquette* (1901), cites "the fine shades of meaning conveyed in such behavior," acknowledging that "a very punctilious man accounts it the better form to carry in his hat and cane when making a first formal call, because to leave them behind implies a familiarity with the house and hostess he dares not claim." Etiquette books, by their very nature, represent an admittedly conservative reading of social mores, and Holt's probably described the norms of the previous decade.

In displaying their cherished objects, the Victorians were orderly and opinionated. After all, something as important as the decoration of one's home was not likely to go unregulated. Just as there was a definite security and comfort in knowing how one was expected to think or behave, so the Victorians thought certain objects belonged in certain rooms and had to be arranged and displayed in

The reverence for ancestry and family ties was expressed in myriad family photographs, *above and opposite,* that collectors enjoy displaying today.

certain ways. Fine oil paintings, for example, should never be hung in the hallway; prints, family portraits (as distinct from other paintings), and statuary were best there, set on brackets or in shadowy little niches. The Victorians were never arbitrary in their pronouncements, though. Consistently and conscientiously they explain to us their logic and reasoning, which, in the light of the 19th century's intricate theories of the linkage between behavior and design, usually made surprisingly good 19th-century sense. Those with true artistic sensibility would immediately be able to realize that the narrowness of a typical hallway, and the brief time one spent in it before being led to the parlor, made it an unsuitable place for the scrutiny of fine oils.

The Victorians may have fully understood the narrative power that objects had in their society, but they also realized that interesting objects, interestingly displayed, were essential for the comfortable lived-in feeling they wanted in their homes. Objects were personal; they promoted a lively backdrop for social interaction. Objects warmed their grandiose spaces, took away the forbidding chill of high-ceilinged parlors and dark snaking hallways. A home without its cluttery little tabletop or manteltop arrangements, was considered bereft of the essential personal touch, unwelcoming and perhaps even willfully neglected. In L. T. Meade's *Sweet Girl Graduate,* the "bare ugliness" of charity student Priscilla Peel's room is a contemptible shortcoming in the eyes of the other students, who patronized local shops to "buy tables

and chairs and pretty artistic cloths and little whatnots of all descriptions" in order to make their rooms homelike. "The electric light [in Priscilla's room] was turned on, revealing the bareness and absence of all ornament of the apartment; a fire was laid in the grate but not lit."

What is interesting, of course, is the Victorian concept of bareness compared to our own as the young lady's room is further described as follows: "The furniture was excellent of its kind. A Turkey carpet covered the center of the floor, the boards round the edge were stained and brightly polished. In one corner of the room was a little bed made to look like a sofa by day with a Liberty cretonne covering. A curtain of the same shut away the wardrobe and washing apparatus. Just under one of the bay windows stood . . . a writing table, and a bookcase at the top, and a chest of drawers to hold linen below. Besides this there was a small square table for tea in the room and a couple of chairs." Amazingly, concludes the author: "The whole effect was undoubtedly bare."

Although today we are far from that 19th-century extreme, objects and collectibles still bring a feeling of warmth to a room. Collections of Victoriana *still* carry associations and meanings beyond their physical manifestations; *still* endow a room with history, personality, emotion, and warmth. Because of the special nature of Victoriana, the original 19th-century decorative principles for showing objects and collections to greatest effect are often the best starting point for effective arrangement and display today.

Victorian asymmetry is apparent in the offbeat irregularity and varying heights and sizes of the arrangement *opposite,* which pairs contemporary candleholders with rare Aesthetic-era porcelains. The quirky unpredictability of the "patterning" of Victorian crazy quilts follows the same decorative principle. *Below,* a collection of antique crib quilts.

ASYMMETRY Victorians in the later part of the 19th century embraced the charm of asymmetry in decorative arrangements as opposed to the classical balance popular in the first quarter of the century. This accords with the Victorians' eclectic taste, their affection for the odd and unpredictable assortment of furnishings and objects, seemingly haphazardly put together. *Seemingly* is the key word here—for the jumble of apparently crazed clutter we associate with Victorian collecting was in fact a careful assemblage, thoughtfully arranged. Their delight in the effect of the random mix was childishly genuine. Part of their fascination with creating albums and scrapbooks, for example, to which artistic friends and family were encouraged to contribute, was the anticipation of the unexpected—the charming unpredictability of what might appear on the next page. The same principle applied to the appeal of the collagelike scrap screens they so admired; and similarly, the lure of crazy quilts. The quirky randomness, the irreverent disregard for pattern and balance, was viewed as fresh and modern—even avant-garde—by the Victorians. Since they were ruled by rigid codes in so many other areas of their lives, they were drawn to the dashing jumble of the asymmetrical arrangement.

CLUSTERING While some reform-oriented tastemakers professed an admiration for the simplicity and sparseness of what they called the Japanesque style, the reality of the Victorian home was another matter entirely. Clustering—

Clustering—*opposite*, on an
artfully arranged dresser, and
in various groupings, *this page*
—was perhaps the essential
element in Victorian arrangement and display.

grouping many objects closely together in a magnificent mixed-up assembly— was a key feature of Victorian display.

The Victorians had several reasons for crowding so many disparate objects, so much bric-a-brac, together on one small surface or space. Aside from the social and cultural ones (more objects meant more wealth), there was also a psychological basis for clustering. Victorians, their eyes accustomed to multilayered, multipatterned, filled-to-overflowing interiors, had an unusually high capacity for absorbing ornamentation, far more sophisticated than ours is today. Empty spaces seemed barren, strange, even dull, with few objects on which to rest one's eyes, few to engage and hold one's interest.

A goodly number of objects in assorted heights and sizes, for example, were needed to make an effective showing against the rich patterning of Victorian walls and upholstery; otherwise, too few objects would fail to hold their own against the overpowering strength of the architecture and furnishings. One slender silver candlestick, for example, would be lost in the marvelous confusion of pattern, color, upholstery, and trim. A grouping of three, four, or five, though chunkier and more ornate, mixed with other collectibles was able to make a statement. Thickly clustered groups of objects tended to reinforce the identity of the individual item; interspersing objects of varying heights and sizes (and separating matched pairs) in the arrangement provided (and still does provide) a more visually interesting effect.

mood. "Shadows about the room greatly add to its charm," was the considered opinion of *The Household*. It was felt that candles in brass candlesticks, placed at odd intervals, also gave life and sparkle to wall decorations in the room.

MANTELSCAPES Upon the parlor mantel were arranged what are today known as "mantelscapes," very much the focal point for collecting in the American Victorian home. Mantels overflowed with objects of all kinds, but certain items appear again and again as central and appropriate icons.

During mid-century, for example, and for some time after, a handsome clock

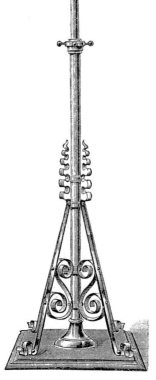

LIGHTING Another—and practical—reason for clustering objects was that in order to be seen, collections had to be fixed within small spheres of available light. Oil lamps, gaslight, sconces on the walls, new lights installed into the newel posts of one's stairs, and table lamps everywhere enabled one to show off one's home after sunset, to entertain long into the night. Plenty of gilding and mirrors helped, too, with reflection doubling the glow.

Even with the Victorians' warm golden lamplight their objects or rooms were far from illuminated. More important were the play of shadows, flickering candlelight, and an artistic regard for

Victorian lighting encouraged the clustering of collectibles on tabletops and other surfaces. Lamps with fanciful fringed or fabric shades, like the example *above left*, or painted globes such as the one *above*, provided the illumination. The Victorians also had fancy floor lamps, like the copper and brass design with a silk and lace shade, *left*.

The mantelscape in my dining room features a mix of favorite objects: old and new toy furniture (particularly chairs)—some pieces from the late 19th century, others from the early 20th—a framed bit of braided hair art, and engravings of Victorian dogs.

occupied the mantel place of honor, usually flanked by two candlesticks or with prism-dangling girandoles. Words of disparagement from some tastemakers did not discourage the practice (while appropriate, a clock was hardly that interesting or significant as an object). Clarence Cook, for instance, scorned the clock and candlestick trio, believing that the mantel should be home only to the most "beautiful and chosen things—the most beautiful that the family purse can afford... things to lift us up, to feed thought and feeling, things we are willing to live with, to have our children grow up with and that we can never become tired of because they belong alike to nature and to human-

ity." As for a clock, hardly. To Cook's mind, nothing less than a copy of some noble work of art, a famous painting, or a cast of a great sculpture would do. Also, a few "pleasant little things" would do— a Japanese bronze, a Satsuma cup, an Etruscan vase, a beautiful shell, or a piece of Venetian glass. Even objects as simple as tumblers of fresh roses, quaintly painted gourds, or candlesticks with real candles, made for an enticing and eclectic assortment.

As the era progressed, and tastes became increasingly eccentric (or artistic, if you will), the mantel became a repository for what were termed *worthy* collectibles, those with the most cultural, artistic, and economic significance, rather than what was termed trivial bric-a-brac. By the 1870s and 1880s, for example, mid-century–domed arrangements of wax or shellwork flowers and card racks (which held calling cards) were discarded. In fashion-conscious homes, these visiting card racks were moved to the hallway (which made it all the easier for nosy visitors to do a little social snooping, riffling through the assembled cards, to assess their friends' popularity and social standing). Domed arrangements were relocated to a corner table, an extra pedestal, or étagère.

What blossomed instead on the mantel was an elaborate assortment of opulent, often foreign, objects, a plum-pudding 19th-century richness and air of luxury the only common denominator. A stuffed peacock, tail feathers sweeping down to the carpeting, might jostle elegant Sèvres china plates, candelabra, exotically carved vases, bits of jade, and an inlaid music box. A marble or Parian bust was also a constant, and candlesticks "with real candles" were looked on with favor. In the late 1880s, one of the more influential magazines, *The Decorator & Furnisher,* specifically points out that tall objects, presumably candlesticks or lamps, tend to look well when placed in the middle of the mantel and on its ends. Also during those years, the unattractive "coldness" of a white-marble mantel was nearly always dressed in drapery, usually a velvet lambrequin.

Another distinguishing feature of the mantelscape was the architectural development of the overmantel—the ele-

Collections of all kinds, at home on today's Victorian mantels: *Top,* old-fashioned pitchers and a rustic basket convey a country feeling on the parlor mantel of this Victorian inn; *above,* a collection of vintage purses displayed on an oak mantel, ca. 1882.

The mantelscape, *top,* combines objects of nature—pinecones, trailing greenery—with drapery and a collection of photographs; *left and above,* two mantels rich with original tilework and carved ornamentation.

gant and picturesque arrangement of built-in shelves and brackets topping the mantel and usually surrounding a central mirror. Its appearance was but another concession to the all-consuming collecting imperative: a supersize "curio cabinet" for rich and dramatic display.

Mantels were considered so important in the home, such a central focus for collecting as well as for family life, that if one had no mantel, say, in a bedroom, one was encouraged to create a makeshift version. What was a mantel, after all, but a shelf? "If there be no mantel in the room, a shelf and bracket, arranged with mantel draperies, may be added to the chamber at a cost which is but trifling when its uses and attractions are considered," the Victorians were advised by *The Household* and other guidebooks during the 1880s.

TABLETOPS A profusion of tables, big and small, was an integral part of Victorian style—from the parlor's center table, surrounded by chairs drawn up in a cozy, conversational way, to small tables of all kinds set up in corners, adjacent to big easy chairs, in the hallway, holding the calling-card tray and other small items, even on a stair landing. These surfaces were custom-made to hold meticulously arranged still lifes of flowers, crafts and objects, often centered by the glow of lamplight.

While waiting in the parlor for one's host or hostess, the study of such a still life could easily occupy a guest's thoughts and attention. A tabletop still life might have a theme of sorts, all the

items related in some way; more often it was made up of an unrelated but interesting mix of objects.

On a tabletop, the Victorians found that any group of unrelated items would unite into a collection if grounded or bordered—arranged on a silver tray, a mirror, a piece of fabric or lace, an antimacassar, a dresser scarf, or the like. Without such a base, the objects tend to "float." Collectors today will agree: objects look more finished, more a collection when anchored on a surface of some sort.

The Victorians also liked to combine their tabletop still lifes with a backdrop of wall-hung art to form what was known as an art unit. These art-unit vignettes consisted of carefully arranged tabletop collectibles, against a wall of pictures and prints, all arranged fairly close together (clustered), because of the limitations of the lighting of the day. Occasionally a picture or two wouldn't be hung at all, but simply propped up on the table for what the Victorians felt was an interesting, casual effect.

VIGNETTES
More than a tabletop, less than a room—that's the nature of what might be called the Victorian vignette. For those coping with the chilly conditions of contemporary construction, the Victorian vignette, while not as satisfying as an entire interior, can go a long way toward curbing the hunger for a more complete banquet of Victorian style.

The Victorian vignette consists of a carefully clustered arrangement of smaller 19th-century collectibles and keepsakes anchored by a larger piece of

These tiny 19th-century shoes, *opposite and top,* **some with hidden compartments for sweets, are the focal point of this collector's elegant tabletop arrangement, while a froth of handworked lace provides an appropriate base for a collection of vintage books, photographs and objects,** *above.*

furniture—a cupboard, a chair, a cabinet. Draped or skirted tabletops are the most frequent focal points of a vignette, but an unused cupboard, or even an awkward corner or bare wall can also work. And even the most uncompromising of high-rises, devoid of detail, can take on the personal charm we associate with the 19th century when fitted out with one or two of these displays.

Most Victorian-style interiors, in fact, are simply made up of a few of these clustered vignettes combined—a romantic dressing table with its old-fashioned purses and perfume bottles; a mirror and marble-topped table framed by two draped parlor windows; a charming low table set for tea. A set of old-fashioned ceramic canisters can add a touch of nostalgia to a modern apartment kitchen. The drape of an antique glove over a jewelry box, or a cluster of vintage accessories can help shift the tone of a room back in time, as the eye takes in these settings, first as a whole, then one at a time.

Photographs of authentic 19th-century interiors (William Seale's classic *The Tasteful Interlude* is probably the best source) reveal that the look is well grounded in tradition. Small eclectic furniture groupings—the odd table, the extra chair, the cozy settee—were very much the preferred parlor arrangement. *The House Beautiful* (1878) emphasized the importance of accessories as "the ornament of life—casts, pictures, engravings, bronzes, books [are the] chief nourishers in life's feast." To another tastemaker collectibles were "the very things that add life . . . to a room."

Tablescapes can include a re-
markable number of small objects: *Above,* a stunning
collection of tiny treasures, ornamental pill boxes and frames;
right, in the home of the same
collector, the ultimate clustered
tabletop, all family photos. *Opposite:* The Victorian vignette
—a corner of a room, complete
in itself, with a comfortable
19th-century chair, beadwork
footstool, lamp, and cherished
collectibles all around.

Just as the Victorians created these vignettes to personalize the look of their homes, so today, they can be an essential element in reproducing a 19th-century feeling in a more contemporary space. Not all the items in a vignette have to be old, however, in order to create an old-time feeling, but they do have to have the proper look. In a kitchen, for example, the distinctive lettering and bright colors of antique tin and tea boxes can create a charming shelf-top vignette, whether the items are reproductions or genuine. Art Deco pieces often have enough of a compatible, ornamental quality to complement 19th-century collections. To avoid a musty, museum look, it's a good idea to mix in a few absolutely new pieces. Modern color photographs among the old, a basket of apples, greenery, or flowers all add a sense of real life to a still life and help eliminate fussiness.

Corners can be significant when positioning the vignette. Well aware of the lack of space in city apartments, which were just starting to proliferate during the 1880s, Clarence Cook, in his most famous work, *The House Beautiful* (1878), looked on the corner as an excellent way to preserve space by keeping the floors free of furniture. Using built-in corner cupboards to house glass, china, curios, objects, shells, and so forth, was a favorite way in the old-fashioned days, he wrote. So, too, today.

Vignettes can also be created in unexpected places. An otherwise dull hallway can become more interesting to walk through day after day if it is hung with a collection of sentimental needle-

Victorian architectural effects were often put in the service of display, as in the hallway niche, *above,* a common Victorian convention designed to showcase a piece of art or sculpture. In this collector's home, a Rogers Group, one of the most popular art collectibles of the 19th century, is featured. *Opposite:* The elegant Victorian étagère is a piece of furniture created solely for displaying bric-a-brac.

work and samplers. The sides of a stairwell, the space over a door, the kitchen windowsill are all forgotten spaces waiting to be filled.

In a completely modern apartment, without any architectural features to help set the mood, odd pieces of Victorian furniture can serve as the "anchor" for a vignette. Old curio cabinets (the Victorians looked on these as great space-savers for apartment dwellers), hutches, glassed-in cabinets, printer's boxes with their tiny cubbies to hold miniature knickknacks, all supply good display surfaces for an apartment.

FURNITURE   Victorian collecting is also underscored by the furniture and domestic architecture of their homes. The accelerated pace of collecting brought about a change in the very shape and purpose of Victorian furniture—a pressing need for shelving and display surfaces. In some cases, entirely new pieces came into existence; in other cases, standard pieces were altered to better accommodate the bulk of fashionable accumulation.

Among the many new kinds of multishelved furniture in city parlors was the elegant étagère. Along with its country cousin, the whatnot, a sometimes rickety little corner piece, it was invented solely for the purpose of showcasing Victorian bric-a-brac. Clarence Cook notes with appreciation "the fine name(s) which we have given to a set of shelves which gives us an opportunity to display many pretty things in the way of bric-a-brac...."

Cabinets and display cases occupied nearly every Victorian parlor. *Top, from left:* A built-in butler's pantry, a dining room cabinet, a pie safe. *Second row:* Collectibles in the kitchen—a cabinet filled with vintage toys; a display of 19th-century pressed glass and transfer-printed ware in a cupboard. *Left:* Collectibles on cabinet tops.

Collectors' choices include, *top, from left:* A multishelved bedroom mirror; an ebonized Aesthetic cabinet, once a parlor piece, today holds jewelry and accessories; and a marble-topped dresser. *Second row:* A quaint collection in a bathroom cabinet; a tall-mirrored dresser; and, in a study, glass doors display old-time music rolls. *Right:* a Welsh cupboard in a kitchen holds *porcelain de Paris.*

A golden oak china-closet-cum-server, *above,* a popular combination piece, displays this collector's silver and china in a Victorian-style dining room. *Right:* A handsome Renaissance Revival dresser in another collector's guest room. *Opposite:* The lure of drapery everywhere, from copiously canopied beds to lace-embellished windows, all, not coincidentally, echoed in the women's fashions of the day—such as the bustled walking and evening dresses here, from *Harper's Bazar* (ca. 1883).

Servers and sideboards were huge expansive surfaces, top-heavy now, with cubbies and shelves (sometimes mirrored in the back, so that the collection appeared more abundant than it really was), curio cabinets, china cupboards, and dressers with little shelves and glove boxes for trinkets and treasures were all avidly collected. Even old cupboards were creatively recycled. One way to achieve the right effect was to remove the doors from an "old-fashioned cupboard," paint the inside deep red (or line it with a red cloth), and top the shelves with leather pinked on the edges and tacked in place with brass upholstery nails. "Into this alcove or recess put all the quaint vases, china, brass ornaments, anything odd or pretty," the Victorians were told. And put the whole setup in the sitting room.

In addition to fireplace overmantels, mantels also would have had inset compartments for vases or grooves to steady fragile decorative plates. Also, wall niches (designed by Victorian architects specifically to hold sculpture) and built-in cupboards of all kinds came into being. Built-in furniture (library shelves, sideboards, and servers in particular) was especially popular in Queen Anne–style homes, where the odd, asymmetrically shaped rooms required something of a custom fit. "Many a wet day was spent by Mina and me in exploring . . . cupboards, passages and dark corners," wrote M. V. Hughes in her memoirs of the 1880s. She remembers rooting out treasures from old wardrobes, cabinets, great deep closet cupboards in the bedrooms, and even a cavernous cellar cupboard running underneath the breakfast parlor. All these built-in units had a single purpose—to store and display the masses of objects that the Victorians now proudly called their own.

DRAPERY On all of these shelved pieces, on the mantels and the tabletops, throughout the home, objects were traditionally clustered in certain ways. For one thing, the surfaces on which they rested would have been scrupulously draped. The well-documented Victorian distaste for bare surfaces—which sometimes seems to border on obsession—demanded it. As with the blankness of a wall without its covering of wallpaper or paint, a marble-top table, without its dressing of lace, tapestry, or velvet, without some sort of dresser scarf, shawl, or tidy had a disconcertingly cold and unfinished look.

Victorian women's lives were so closely identified with the home sphere that a curious relationship sprung up between women's fashion and home furnishings—a relationship that in some aspects persists to this day. At its height, the flounces and furbelows, the draperies, valences, and trim that disguised the contours of the Victorian window, for example, resembled nothing so much as the flounced and draped dresses of the period. Upholstery fabrics and dress fabrics often shared the same patterns. Paisley shawls, very much the status symbol for women during the early-Victorian decades, moved, as the era progressed, from draping feminine shoulders to draping the corners of a plump settee or easy chair, while fringed dresser scarves, silk piano

shawls, and other coverings modestly concealed the physical shapes of tables, chairs, mantels, and footstools. Although the myth of the Victorians shrouding piano legs in petticoats was just that—a myth—bare contours, whether table leg or lady's leg, were jarring to Victorian eyes. Fabrics dressed up the functional parts of furniture as they did a female form.

Marble-topped tables, of course, were nearly always draped: a crimson velvet covering or one in tapestry was considered a better backdrop for objects on display. Even today, in an otherwise well-furnished Victorian-style room, marble without draping can have a startling effect. Mantels, like windows, frequently wore elaborate curtainings called lambrequins. One household guide recommends the following beshrouded scene to fashion-conscious home decorators: a bit of rich material or an old crepe shawl hung on an easel, draping a picture; a Roman scarf on a shelf to enliven a dark corner; a painted or embroidered silk curtain hung beneath a bracket supporting a bust; Persian chair scarves; plaques hung against "rich background(s) of velvet or silk"—all in the same room.

For good measure, one could drape an embroidered curtain in front of a low bookcase. Although this was quite the fashion in 1882, it was regarded dubiously, since it wouldn't allow "even a glimpse of the books one is so proud of." On occasion, it was said, a bare statue might have worn a concealing bit of gauze —the very last word in gentility and refined taste.

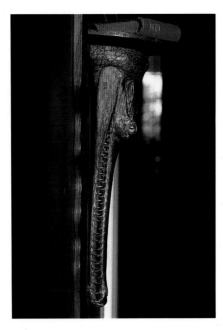

Small, wall-hanging shelves, *above and opposite,* provide still further space for the display of objects.

WALLSCAPES More advice than can possibly be recorded was bandied about on the crucial arrangement of pictures, paintings, prints, and objects on Victorian walls. On the whole, though, what was promoted was a varied display —not just paintings or prints, but objects and greenery mixed in. "A bracket here and there beneath a picture with a pot of ivy can form a graceful frame to a portrait of a loved one or engraving or chromo," one writer advised. Brackets holding vases and sculptures, quaint little wall shelves, hanging cabinets, even Victorian wall pockets—clever little catch-alls that provided handy storage for letters, keys, and other household gee-gaws—made the wallscapes something to admire and enjoy.

The hanging shelves, cupboards, and curio cabinets, often ebonized in the Aesthetic style, were some of the most popular additions to the Victorian wall grouping. The shelves primarily held unusual pieces of china, small brass vases, jades, ivories, or other collectibles of an Aesthetic bent. Pearly shells or a charming carved box were also appropriate. Sometimes such a hanging wall shelf, filled with china and brass, could be placed above the parlor mantel instead of an overmantel.

Style books of the period reveal that the Victorians liked to use every available inch of wall space, as well as the backs of doors and the sides of stair walls, to show off the furious patterns of their wallpapers. When one hung a picture over a door, though, it was imperative that it not be a small watercolor "or anything of

that kind so that its beauty is entirely lost on anybody under eight feet tall." The pictures that worked best over a door were felt to be still lifes of flowers and fruits.

Another addition to the wallscape was a touch of nature. Oats and grasses, for example, might be tied with a band of wide satin ribbon, or ferns and cattails adorned with a bow, and placed over or under a picture for what was thought a simple and unaffected bit of ornamentation. Pampas plumes were also popular. A large plume, mixed with peahen feathers and tied with a peacock-blue or green ribbon, might gracefully bedeck the space over a door, under a picture, in a bare corner, or on an easel or mirror. The same plumes, placed in a vase, could go on the mantel or fill up an empty corner that otherwise had escaped decorative notice.

The Victorians had the habit of hanging paintings, pictures, and prints on braided cords or wires, from picture rails about a foot from the top of the ceiling, at an odd, characteristically slanted angle (usually tilted forward). Hanging pictures on cords, with a tassel or bow as ornament, is one of the more charming customs that has been revived today in Victorian and non-Victorian interiors alike. In addition to the ornamental quality, the use of the picture rail also prevented damage to walls. Hanging a picture from one single point—the cords or wires forming an inverted **V**—was regarded by some tastemakers as a distraction from the artistic arrangement; they preferred the picture suspended from two separate points. As for the old-fashioned

An assembly of Victorian-style wallscapes features a variety of collections, including a rustic-influenced "hall tree" of vintage antlers, rare Currier & Ives images still in their original frames, vintage samplers, English animal prints scaling a staircase, and more. *Overleaf left:* In closeup, framed needlecraft, old currency, and other collectibles united in a Victorian wallscape; *right,* a time-worn sampler, cherished then . . . and now.

forward tilt we associate with Victorian pictures, some say it was to reduce glare, and to make it easier to examine the brush strokes. Pictures were often hung high to take advantage of the height of most Victorian rooms too. The tilt therefore provided a better angle for viewing.

Just as the Victorians collected things with special meanings that are not remembered today, it's interesting to note which of their collected objects have survived, regardless of their original interest, and why.

Many of the articles the Victorians regarded as precious, aesthetically beautiful, or intellectually or culturally worthwhile, for example, we appreciate for reasons they hardly would have suspected. They would probably be surprised at our pleasure in the idiosyncratic designs of their common silverplate: what we read into an object often increases its value to us as collectors, and silverplate is particularly indicative, particularly Victorian in design and material, of the age. Or by our appreciation of mundane household items—tin and old kitchen utensils, purely functional things, never intended to be collected. Today, we value them for what they say about the era, rather than for any intrinsic beauty of design or quality of materials.

In addition, although the Victorians would expect us to revere their handcrafted items, they probably would be surprised, if not gently offended, that we collect them not as the objects of beauty and refinement they were intended to be, but as cultural artifacts, oddities of another, less harried time.

Jesus my saviour and my Lord

To thee I lift mine eyes

Teach and instruct me by thy word

And make me truly wise

Cherished Objects

■

PORTFOLIO OF HOMES

5

PUTTING IT ALL TOGETHER

Does an affinity for Victoriana mean a commitment to a single style of decorating? Not necessarily so. That's where, beginning with this chapter, the following Victorian "Portfolio of Homes" fits in, illustrating how collectors live with and enjoy their collections in many rich and diverse ways.

Because of the eclectic nature of Victoriana, and because of its abundance —such an astonishing lot of stuff produced over such a very long span of time —no single design formula really defines its use: even at the outset, its reach was long, its appeal generous, diversified. Just as in the 19th century, when Victorian objects and furnishings adorned one man's exotic "Persian palace" or another's picturesque Gothic cottage, and its wicker created the homeness and informality we associate with lazy summer living and a nostalgic "front-porch" charm, then and now, so living with 19th-century antiques, collections, and memorabilia is very much a matter of personal expression. Its very eclecticism—that broad mix—is what Victorian collecting is all about.

One of the most gratifying things about collecting Victoriana is how well the era's furnishings and accessories blend with those of other periods. Its richly ornamental qualities are compatible with so many other styles: as an offbeat counterpoint to the spareness of, say, a room filled with a collection of Shaker pieces; lending a romantic sophistication to a country parlor; taking the chill off the edges of a contemporary loft.

It is with this variety in mind that collectors today can look at Victoriana anew—from those who showcase their collections in painstakingly assembled period-perfect rooms to those who prefer their collections to set a tone rather than re-create an exact period.

Most strong collections of Victoriana tend to manifest themselves in one of five major directions. On the pages that follow is a look at those five—and how a group of very inventive collectors have interpreted them. While most collectors of Victoriana cross lines, creatively blending two or more of the themes, these divisions illustrate the strongest patterns of collecting today, making it easier to understand collections that merge with their settings into a harmonious whole.

IN THE GRAND MANNER

Collecting "in the grand manner" requires a certain panache, a willingness to mix the French Rothschilds with both Queen Victoria and Gypsy Rose Lee. In this approach to Victoriana, the point of view is both urban and urbane—a polished and masterful blend, with a concentration on the finer elements: beautifully proportioned 19th-century furniture, rich fabrics, lavish draperies, sprinkled with sophisticated and unexpected Victorian objects and artifacts.

All this can be found in this fanciful little Victorian house, with French towers and Eastlake accents, arrayed in plum and gilt coloring, which sits demurely on a quiet San Francisco street. Built in 1885 by a French family for their two sons (it still has the original two entrances with nine rooms on either side), its storybook architecture harks back to the glories of Notre Dame, jumbled with the Eastlake influences so popular in America at that time.

Inside, thanks to collectors Don Van Derby and Don B. Liles, a worldly sophistication reigns. Nineteenth-century Staffordshire figures with hand-painted bisque faces, dressed in Scottish folk costumes (ca. 1875) recall the height of Queen Victoria's Balmoral period. Wrapping the upper perimeters of the front

Below: Sensuous shapes, serious furniture. The elaborately carved medallion-back settee in gleaming rosewood is Dutch, but similar to American Rococo Revival settees sought after in the 1850s and 1860s. Then, when the style was new, its rich carving and fashionable, rollicking curves made it an immediate symbol of wealth and style. On the walls, 19th-century landscapes and gilded "pineapple" brackets.

Opposite: In the front parlor, a strong French influence prevails, with two unmatched Victorian chairs flanking the blue marble mantel inlaid with gold leaf. Above it, a gilt Rococo Revival mirror. The sculpture in the foregound (on an 1850s American marble-top table) is titled *The Wounded Gaul* and carved in alabaster, a material the Victorians loved for its purity, as well as for the very romantic sound of the word itself.

parlor is a lavish chintz border, originally designed for Ferrier, the French Rothschild home. An exquisite silver Art Nouveau mirror was once owned by Gypsy Rose Lee. Overall, there is a civilized sheen about the furnishings, the collections, and the manner of living they express.

These jewel-like interiors and the juxtaposition of objects are the result of decades of refined collecting. What is unusual is that each individual piece—the elegant mid-century rosewood furniture and grandiose mirrors, the witty antique ivories and jades, the procession of eyebrow-raising late-century Aubrey Beardsley illustrations, each beautifully framed, advancing down the hall—stands on its own. Nothing was collected merely to fill a space.

The acquisition of key pieces—in fact, pieces later to become the cornerstones of the collection—even spurred the renovation of the house itself in the collectors' desire to create lavish but comfortable "backgrounds" to dramatize the objects at their best.

The elegant Rococo Revival settee in the back parlor, for example, was purchased at auction in the mid-1960s in deplorable condition. Later it was reupholstered in the unusual, light-catching green/gold Chinese silk damask you see here. The painted walls came next; their green/gold character was chosen to enhance the fabric's shading.

Then there is the luxe of faux finishes—an opulent trompe-l'oeil marble dado and innovative combination of wallpapers—complementing the elegant as-

Above: a particularly graceful example of Victorian hair art in a delicate oval frame. *Left:* This unusual Art Nouveau light fixture, cast bronze and American-made, with glass calla lily shades, hangs in the bedroom. During the 1890s, the Victorians envisioned, in free-flowing shapes like these, a new, untraditional—and seductive—celebration of nature. *Opposite:* To set off this shallow dining-room alcove the owners used a deep Pompeian red paint, a shade the Victorians admired for its richness and drama. The space is further divided by the hanging lambrequin. Balloon-back chairs, shaped to accommodate feminine fashion, are typical of the period from 1850 to 1870.

semblage of choice 19th-century objects in the dining room, from old-fashioned portraits and silver and china, to rare late-19th-century European ivories.

While Van Derby and Liles bring an artist's eye, a connoisseur's discrimination to the fine points of their collection, it is the contrast of their collection of Victorian oddities with the unabashed elegance of the interiors that sets it apart: an antique rhinoceros foot that serves as a humidor; a delicate oval hair-art memento (ca. 1882); an emu egg (ca. 1904), inscribed and mounted as a Victorian presentation piece, once belonging to an officer in the Australian army. These and others are the sort of quirky pieces that charmed our 19th-century ancestors and that Van Derby and Liles take particular pride in today. "We enjoy knowing what these things must have meant to people then in order for them to have created them," they explain. One piece, the hoof of a pony made into an inkwell, is particularly endearing. Mounted in silver, it's inscribed *In loving memory of Gringo, a faithful friend, Christmas 1911.* "In our throwaway society, we allow things to disappear from our lives," they point out. "We don't permit ourselves to memorialize as the Victorians did."

It is precisely that tolerant and sentimental fondness these collectors have for the idiosyncratic side of the century, combined with their luxurious appreciation of each individual object, that warms this very grand collection into a comfortable and personal home. Few collectors of Victoriana or of any period are able to achieve such a natural style.

Above: Victorian oddities—a humidor created from a rhinoceros's foot (ca. 1900), a rhino tooth, a deer-footed letter opener, a Scottish badger's foot, a carved walrus tusk (American scrimshaw), polished curved horns, a black box used to hold pen nibs, and an inscribed and mounted pony's foot (ca. 1911). *Opposite:* Carved ivories and porcelain figurines form a collection on this draped and fringed tabletop.

IN A NOSTALGIC WAY

The warm, nostalgic approach to Victoriana is perhaps the most familiar look to all of us—a look suggested by faded sepia photographs, family picnics, cozy wicker, and vintage lace. Done well, it is probably the most livable, most comfortable approach to collecting. It is a type of Victoriana, though, that can easily fall into period cliché. To keep it elevated to its highest level, one needs a clear sense of historical perspective; to lend it a rich patina of authenticity, a good eye.

What strikes one first about the Clendenon residence in southern California is its homey and authentic feeling. The family actually relocated this eclectic, asymmetric, "somewhat Queen Anne" home (ca. 1882) from its original site a few blocks away, and settled it comfortably at its present location. There it rests, looking at home with the landscape, just as if it had been there for the last century or so.

Although the dedication to authenticity is certainly here—the Clendenon parlor is a scene straight from America's 1880s—the comfort, the old-fashioned mix of furnishings and collections set a sophisticated tone, far outweighing any possible period mustiness.

"What has happened in the past is how we learn about the future," com-

Opposite: **A draped table holds a helmet-shaped leaded glass lamp, old books, new letters, and part of an eleven-piece 19th-century pottery smoking set. The Victorians would have approved the greenery positioned in the windows, which filter and diffuse the light, creating a play of light and shadow, and softening the contours of the furniture.** *Above:* **Daughter Ivy, four years old, in antique whites with lilacs.** *Overleaf:* **Realizing the importance of drapery in setting a period mood, the Clendenons have dressed the tables in their parlor with vintage textiles, and set a lamp to illuminate each circle of objects. The profusion of light fixtures visible in the room—overhead chandelier, mantel sconces, floor lamp, table lamps—is true to Victorian tradition.**

ments Alan Clendenon on the couple's enthusiasm for all things Victorian—from the contents of their home to the antique cars he restores. On walking into the parlor, the visitor can't help but think how easy it would be to settle into one of the big, tufted chairs, to prop one's feet on a waiting footstool, leaf through one of the old albums, gaze at the niches in the overmantel, each one filled with a small treasure. Here is the Victorian America that so many of us imagine—tucked away in a corner of the 20th century.

Alan and LaDel Clendenon credit the vintage photographs in Joseph Byron's *New York Interiors at the Turn-of-the-Century* and *The Tasteful Interlude* as their models and guideposts to displaying what they have collected over the years: Rose-painted china, old glass, vintage textiles, flagrantly Victorian jardinieres, and an Edison phonograph and cylinders are among the treasure they have assembled. Both have a long-standing interest in the 19th century—he was attracted to the flamboyance of the architecture even as a child—and they have paid particular attention to the art of arrangement, carefully creating clustered vignettes, evocative art units, all with an eye to what they call "balanced clutter"—warm, cloistered, home-centered.

Right: Atop the dining-room
china cabinet sits a collection of
pitchers in silverplate, china,
and cut and pressed glass. The
placement of the framed rose
painting behind the still life
unifies the arrangement, turning it into a Victorian art unit.

Right: This 19th-century berry
set is hand-painted, a medium
widely acclaimed during the
century as one of the decorative
arts. Along with it, other dining
room collectibles—berry spoon
and serving utensils, castor set,
silver beaker, children's mugs.
Opposite: Close-up of a vintage
tassel, a collecting theme
throughout the house.

THE COUNTRY ROMANTIC RETREAT

Above: The solid construction of these photo albums with their heavy metal clasps preserved many of the antique photographs that survive to this day and serves to remind us how highly regarded and precious their contents were. *Opposite:* A country dresser (ca. 1875) holds an old-fashioned leaded glass lamp and "found" pottery bowls. The lace pie safe is a family heirloom.

Victorian romanticism, the lingering charm of a bygone era—this is what comes to mind when one envisions cupboards of delicate linens and laces, ribbon-tied posies and cozy, handmade quilts. To update such old-fashioned charm, collectors are mixing the romance of Victoriana with the easygoing appeal of country. The informality that emerges is a breath of fresh air.

Sharon Abroms of Atlanta has picked up on that country-Victorian mix, but in a very special way. In the confines of a slick, modern structure, she has created a confectionery bower of Victoriana—the ultimate romantic haven. There is nothing cloying about it, though. While the period is evoked with one or two proper Victorian pieces—splendid Heywood Wakefield wicker (ca. 1890), a lushly painted Handel lamp, the gaps are filled in with strictly personal mementos, generous flows of window lace, enriched floral patterns, fresh flowers. Nineteenth-century associations are relaxed a bit, too, mingled with complementary country pieces—a painted pine chest, pretty pottery bowls, a painted Louisiana tin tray. On the whole, while personal style fills the rooms, rather than a concern for any particular period, the romantic charm of the past is everywhere.

Above: As tranquil as a greenhouse, as romantic as a rose garden, this built-on sun room extends the borders of the house into the landscape. Child-size chairs, needlepoint footstools, and a Heywood Wakefield wicker set complete the scene.

Tiny footstools like this cherished pair of round beadwork footstools, *opposite,* an essential part of the Victorian comfort ethic, were found in the parlor.

Preceding pages, left: Buoyed by light from romantic but scantily clad windows, dressed in old lace, the room is enhanced and illuminated by the sun; *right:* The soft, faded colorings of the tapestry, upholstery, and 19th-century needlework pillows hark back to another era.

THE LURE OF VICTORIAN EXOTICA

Exotica fills the homes of so many collectors today, expressing the newly awakened 19th-century interest in accumulating foreign and fanciful treasures. Whether lending a worldly touch to the traditional or showcased in a special, extravagant exotic room of its own, the effect marries Victorian comfort with the titillating contents of a Persian or Turkish bazaar.

Exotica and the worldly air of sophistication it brought to 19th-century homes, is perfectly represented by the fascinating exotic touches in James B. Rogers's New York town house (ca. 1900). This sumptuous beaux-arts manse is crowded with mementos, collectibles, and exotica from all over the world—a motorcycle trip through Alaska's Yukon turned up many of the 19th-century bearskins; another jaunt in northern Thailand resulted in the acquisition of the elephant, carved in teak, tusks and all. Rogers's home can best be described as an interpretive mix—with vignettes of Victoriana all over. But, there is an unmistakable streak of exotica running through its clubby late-Victorian interiors, a tone suggestive of Victorian curiosity and wanderlust. It comes across most strikingly in the unusual rooms on these pages.

Above: **A souvenir Thai teak elephant, framed by crimson cotton damask draperies, stands in close revelry along with an antique screen, comfortably worn leather upholstery, the faded glory of a vintage patchwork quilt, and 19th-century beaded and fringed pillows.**

Opposite: **A glimpse of "the green room," a sitting room/informal dining space, shows off turn-of-the-century metal trunks, symbols of world travel, one atop the other, as a surface for some cherished finds.**

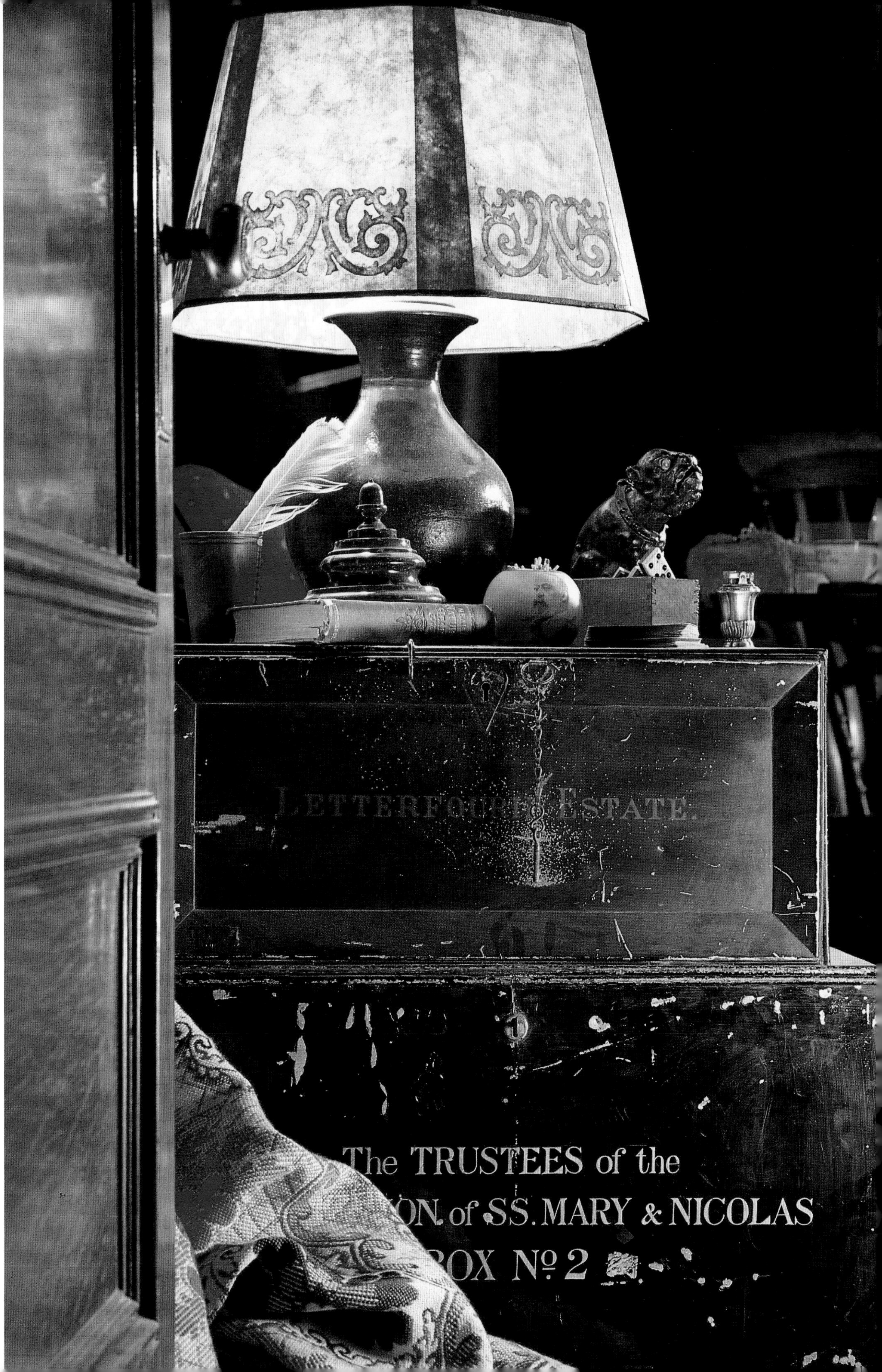
ESTATE.
The TRUSTEES of the
of SS. MARY & NICOLAS
BOX № 2

Above: A prized 19th-century zebra head, a token of Victorian hunting prowess, hangs over the billiard room mantel. *Left:* In a corner, a superb collection of Victorian pillows helps create a casual nook for lounging, reading, and relaxing.

Above: **Exotica overflows the Rogers's billiard room, where all sorts of curiosities set off the massive 19th-century table with its fringed pockets.**
Right: **A bruin umbrella holder, scarfed in college colors, keeps cue sticks and billiard paraphernalia.**

THE MODERN MIX

Old shapes, new setting—that's the core of the modern mix—where virtuoso Victorian pieces with a strong sense of history strut in a cool contemporary environment. Does it work? Unquestionably. Somehow, the Victoriana seems bolder, gutsier, more audacious than ever, almost as if it knows full well it dominates the room. With the innocent, overbearing confidence of a well-loved child, it meets the room head on, all opulence and exultant voluptuary shapes.

It takes a certain sophistication, a willingness to experiment, to pull off the modern mix, as collector Jeanne Golly did in her mid-Manhattan co-op. When

Right: **Herter Brothers daybeds, heaped with cushions and antique pillows, serve as the heart of the living-room arrangement (the mate is on an adjacent wall). The full cushions and lavish upholstery here and elsewhere are intended to soften the hard lines of the apartment, keeping it from appearing stiff and cold. Nineteenth-century chairs surround the ebonized cherry Pottier & Stymus center table (ca. 1865–1870). The rosewood curule chair to the right, upholstered in violet and gold-striped silk, is also Pottier & Stymus, from the same period. A "Turkish" tufted smoking chair with an iron frame,** *left,* **is upholstered in a rich paisley resembling the cashmere paisley shawls that women prized during the 1850s and 1860s. As a contrast to the formality of the furniture, piles of books make unique small "stack" tables.**

Golly says she enjoys "a richly decorated, opulent table. I'm guided by a sense of whimsy and the old Oscar Wilde adage —'Nothing succeeds like excess.' Sometimes I like to see how much I can put on it and still have it work as a table." Here, late-19th-century American etched-glass goblets are combined with modern Andrée Putman china.

she first moved to the space, she intended merely to postpone "real decorating" until she settled in. For the time being, she planned to forego wallpaper, moldings, and draperies and do her best with furniture and accessories alone. Explaining her position to interior designer Dennis Rolland, whose aid she enlisted in putting the new apartment together, she said: "We'll just have to place everything as effectively as possible."

That they did. So much so that Golly ended up keeping it all intact, finding she liked the juxtaposition of her 19th-century, largely Aesthetic-era antiques with the modern architecture.

Golly had long been interested in collecting from the 19th century. Early on, she scouted flea markets and antique shops with knowledgeable friends, learning and developing her eye before she started to buy. Even then, she was attracted to certain pieces of American Victoriana, finding its ornate qualities and its whimsy especially appealing. "I've always been touched by the stories these pieces have to tell, too—who the owners were, why they were built," she adds. Her carved walnut writing desk, for example, made by Herter Brothers for 19th-century entrepreneur Marshall Field (ca. 1880), not only includes such oddments as carved animal feet with toenails, Golly points out, but also incorporates Midwestern themes such as carved and inlaid corn motifs into its design.

Golly wet her feet as a collector buying small things—a 19th-century faux-bamboo (actually maple and tiger maple) cheval mirror (ca. 1880), now in her bedroom, for instance. It wasn't until the 1980s that she got serious, acquiring major pieces for her new home. A pair of Herter Brothers "Sunflower" daybeds (ca. 1874) in honey-colored oak and burled ash, their headboards inset with stylized sunflower motifs, was one of her first major acquisitions. Always intrigued with multipurpose pieces, Golly immediately realized that they would be wonderful settees.

With the help of a friend, antiques dealer Margot Johnson, and Rolland, Jeanne Golly proceeded to assemble an enviable collection, made all the more striking by the wily wit of its arrangement. "I'm a compulsive collector, though," Golly says. "That's why I like the discipline of having a specific period to focus on." Nonetheless, it's her compulsiveness that makes her collection work.

Left: This 19th-century horn chair (ca. 1880–1890), an unexpected touch with the high-style Victorian furnishings— and "wonderful sculpture"—is attributed to San Antonio furniture maker Wenzel Friedrich.

Above: An ebonized cherry Aesthetic-era sideboard cabinet is unexpectedly inlaid with whimsical "pineapples and pussycats hanging off vines," Golly points out. "It's one of those 19th-century pieces that just tickles me. When I look at it, I'm filled with a sense of richness." The unusual footstool (ca. 1880) was made by fastening one cushion atop another.

Above: An antique silk quilt in the Log Cabin pattern, found in Pennsylvania, serves as the base for this tablescape, which grew from odds and ends given to Golly by friends. The books and baby shoes are family heirlooms.

Opposite: A light-filled view of the living room, where unobstructed floor-to-ceiling windows look out on a spectacular view of the city below. Walls, windows, and ceiling remain devoid of ornamentation, leaving the furniture and collectibles, textures and colors, free to command the room.

6

INGLE-MINDED **COLLECTORS**

Within the wide sphere of Victoriana collecting, there are different methods of expression. The very nature of collecting itself makes the pastime far from static. Sometimes a collector might "complete" a collection, actually satiating the craving for certain objects to the fullest, and move on

to something else entirely. When the appetite is lifelong, the hunger incurable, the connection between the collector and the collection becomes permanent.

Along the way, collectors and their collections tend to change. As one learns more about the area of one's choice, tastes may narrow and refine, becoming more selective in inclination. Or they may grow expansive, all-encompassing, depending on the personality and preoccupations of the collector.

The collectors in this section belong to the former category—unusually disciplined, determinedly single-minded people who have concentrated, in-depth, on one or two specific items or categories of Victoriana to the exclusion of all others. Not for them the diversionary poking about in flea markets, dabbling in a little of this, a little of that. For each of these five collectors, even within their larger collections, one special object beguiled them. For one avid specialist, canes and walking sticks are a passion that has filled many hours as well as many corners of his home. For another collector, it is royal commemoratives—on cups and mugs, dishes, platters, pitchers, even tape measures—a tongue-in-cheek but satisfying homage. Somehow, though, whatever their focus—images, objects, furniture, a collection about a person—with all of these collectors, one particular thing seduced them down the road into a very passionate kind of 19th-century collecting, with a very personal vision. Ruling out the grander scheme of Victoriana to focus on its endlessly fascinating details, they have chosen to share an intimate relationship with their 19th-century counterparts.

GAMES PEOPLE PLAYED

The very first game George Sanborn acquired as a collector was the cover of Parker Brothers' "Game of War." "I took it and had it framed because I thought it was one of the nicest things I had ever seen." From then on, Sanborn started buying games—at yard sales, auctions, big flea markets—attracted to the extraordinary beauty and visual strength of the Victorian graphics. A collecting milestone was his purchase at auction of a collection of toys and games, the stock of a long-closed general store. Selling off the multiples, Sanborn found his collecting pastime had become a serious profession.

Today a dealer as well as a collector, Sanborn has developed several theories about people who are particularly attracted to the toys and games of yesteryear. Those who collect 20th-century games, for example, often remember them from childhood: they are collecting the fond associations of those years. Or, the drama of recalling a first train ride can trigger an interest in toy trains or games that feature them. As for collectors of Victorian games, some collect for the rarity of the objects—because of the fragile nature of paper and cardboard, and the hard knocks these games have endured over the years, few have survived in mint con-

Right: **Two picture-block puzzle games (ca. 1860–1870) in George Sanborn's private collection, in their original hinged wooden boxes. Games like these were a relatively new treat for Victorian children and adults, and as a result of frequent playing, boards were often inadvertently cracked or torn and pieces lost over the years. Since games were seldom regarded as precious or collectible by succeeding generations, when they became shabby and worn they were often discarded.** *Below:* **A child's game, "50 Soldiers on Parade," featuring infantry and cavalrymen in brightly colored lithographed uniforms and a cloth American flag, was created in 1913 to inspire nationalism before World War I.**

dition. Then, there are the often strikingly sophisticated graphics, as well as the special slice of social history they represent.

Nineteenth-century games present us with surprising commentary about the life and leisure of the last century. The popular "Innocence Abroad" shows us firsthand the Victorians' keen interest in modes of transportation. In the "District Messenger" game, would-be Victorian entrepreneurs work themselves up the ladder of social and financial success. Early Victorian games tended to emphasize morality. Later, games for amusement and fun became an accepted part of home life: after dinner, family and friends would gather around the dining room table to play. Games began to reflect key 19th-century themes of education and amusement. A card game such as "Authors," a popular game invented in the 1860s, was even approved of by the church as an educational and cultural tool since it allowed members to become familiar with the bestsellers of the day without actually having to read them.

Because the attractive chromolithography of Victorian games tends to have an important appeal for the collector, effective display of a collection is particularly important. Some collectors frame games. Particularly when the game is incomplete, framing is an excellent way to preserve it. Games can also be set on edge to show off their graphics using two rubber bands or tying with string to secure. It's best to avoid stacking, which tends to crush and damage time-worn and crumbling boxes and covers.

A group of games displayed on and in a multidrawered 19th-century cabinet. On top, the wonderful graphics of "The Game of Tight Rope Walking"; "The Game of Trap Shooting," a shooting game of skill; and "Peter Coddles," which was advertised for 10 cents in 1891. Inside the cabinet are smaller card games, known as parlor games. "Snap" included cards with designs suggesting the word *snap* and was widely copied; "Fortune Telling" was considered an inexpensive (15 cents) and amusing ice-breaker for social events; "Old Maid" was the basic card game. (Before copyright laws, games like "Peter Coddles" were reproduced frequently.)

Above: "Noah's Ark," one of
the most popular toys of the
last quarter of the century, had
a religious theme; therefore, it
could be played on Sunday, as
opposed to other amusements,
which were forbidden. This set
probably dates from 1875 to
1890.

Left: The "District Messenger
Boy, or Good Merit Rewarded"
(McLoughlin Brothers, 1886),
cased in a wooden box and sold
for $1.50, was very showy in
design. Players began as mes-
sengers and strove to attain the
presidency of the company.
"Conette" (Milton Bradley Co.)
sold for 25 to 50 cents in the
late 1890s. An adult game of
skill, it was popular at social
gatherings and evening parties.
"Steeplechase," a racing game,
took players across rivers, hurdles, and other obstacles. This
is a McLoughlin Brothers version, which sold for about a
dollar in the late 1890s.

SENTIMENTAL JOURNEY

"We just buy things we like," say Ron and Anne Smith. They were, in fact, purportedly unaware of a particular collecting theme running throughout their West Coast home until a visitor pointed it out. But there they were. In and around the Smiths' romantically eclectic cache of Victoriana—golden oak and lots of family heirloom silver—lurks a quirky, kitschy, tongue-in-cheek bevy of Victorian beauties, their sweet, simpering faces, all dewy-eyed and blushing, painted on plates, cups, saucers and platters, teapots and other genteel domestic goods. In the parlor there is another, up on the wall, gazing soulfully heavenward, while her similarly expressioned sisters purse their cupid's-bow lips from their perch on the china cabinet, below.

How they first happened to collect so many of these hopelessly idealized, achingly sentimental characterizations of virtuous Victorian womanhood, the Smiths are not quite sure. But the affinity is there. Anne Smith, for instance, is a scrap collector, scrap being the whole realm of glossy, 19th-century paper ephemera, particularly the die-cut chromolithographed pictures on trade cards and calling cards, posters and some prints, calendars, and paper dolls. Toward the end of the century, scrap was even avail-

Right: **In the dining room, a 19th-century pot-metal Cupid lamp is one of a number of objects with angel motifs throughout the house. The collection of 19th-century sterling souvenir state spoons (in the Victorian spoon holder) is a family heirloom from Anne Smith's grandmother. The fad for collecting these reached its height during the 1890s and 1900s, with the collectors' goal to acquire a spoon from every state. The Victorian table brush and silver scoop were used to sweep crumbs from the dining-room table.** *Opposite:* **Hand-painted Victorian ladies on vases, pitchers, and plates, along with a sentimental chromolithograph hung from the picture rail, are arranged in the appropriate Victorian art-unit fashion. The dramatic—or rather, melodramatic—quality of the hand-painted expressions is part of their quintessentially Victorian appeal.**

able in sheets of specialized pictorial images, made specifically for Victorian scrap collectors, who liked to fill what became known as scrap books with their favorites. And scrap, of course, tends to feature the same sort of idealized feminine types with the prettiness peaking in the 1880s and 1890s.

Given that, it comes as no surprise that angel and cupid motifs share the Smiths' nest as well. If you like Victoriana, Anne Smith admits, cherubs are hard to avoid.

On a bedroom tabletop covered with lace, this grouping features a painted lady on the left, depicted in what the Victorians felt was a classical spirit, her hair in the late-19th-century version of a Grecian knot of curls.

CITIZEN CANE

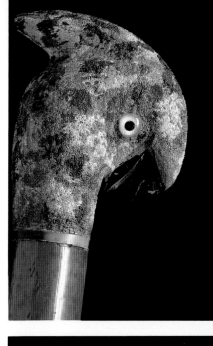

Walking sticks and canes—well over eight hundred of them—fill the corners and scale the walls of collector Stuart White's essentially modern apartment. Although his collection includes samples from other centuries, more than half are Victorian, exemplifying the era that transformed a basically utilitarian object into an aristocratic and gentlemanly accessory, a 19th-century symbol of sartorial elegance. Instead of *using* canes, the Victorians *wore* them, with dash and flair: from the Victorian gold-topped standards, with rosewood or ebony shafts, their knobs either engraved with the owner's initials or inscribed with a date commemorating an event or occasion to quirky mechanical "gadget" canes, products of Victorian technology from the later part of the century which concealed flags, fans, snuff containers, telescopes, binoculars, even daggers. Fashionable bejeweled ladies' canes made their appearance at many a late-century reception, while canes promoting political campaigns, carved with the face of the candidate (Benjamin Harrison in 1880, William Jennings Bryan in 1896) were frequently presented as tokens of back-room esteem.

White's fascination with canes began with his first collecting experience: the purchase of two ornate antique

Opposite: **Expressive carved-bone and -ivory faces and high emotional content characterize this grouping, along with parrots and birds, a favorite Victorian motif.** *Right top:* **A rare French parrot-topped cane is overlaid with minuscule beads.** *Center:* **The silver-skirted woman and silver shoetop are canes that 19th-century men found amusing.** *Bottom:* **These canes, with their richly decorated gold knobs, monograms, and inscriptions, are from the period following the Civil War.**

swords—a Napoleonic officer's sword and a commemorative. Even then he felt a warm glow that piqued his collector's urge. His first real cane was a 19th-century rosewood with a repoussé gold knob and a missing finial. On losing that cane, he began what he calls "a quest" that lasted a year in which he bought more than fifty canes, trying to recover his favorite. "I bought almost every cane of merit I could find," he remembers. In the process, the cane-fancier turned into a true aficionado, tracking down the finest examples wherever he travels, his wife, Carmen, a willing accomplice.

Although White prefers to restore his canes to their original condition, meticulously repairing damages, his collection also includes broken cane handles transformed into magnifying glasses and a small group of knobs and handles tucked away in a drawer. But his real pride, fully polished and restored, is divided into two basic categories. Fine, "dressy" canes stand gracefully in one specially made glass-topped case. This poised grouping, elegant, discreetly jeweled, and glittering, presents a contrast to the clamor and din of his "animated" canes, all topped with heads, faces, animals, and carved ivories. "I call them my menagerie—dragons, alligators, human faces," he says. Here, exotic birds shriek, people seem to shout, jostle, and crowd one another in a turbulent, uproarious, demanding display. They are, White admits, bemused, a visually noisy crew. All in all, the collection speaks loudly about the preoccupations of the past—shared by a collector of today.

Top and opposite: **A group of cane "aristocrats" encrusted with gems, studded with turquoise or mother-of-pearl, in amber, jade, and cloisonné.** *Center:* **A fragile, porcelain-headed cane, probably a lady's dress or court cane.** *Above:* **The "menagerie" encased.**

BARONIAL STRONGHOLD

"There is a masculinity, a boldness to much of the better type of Renaissance Revival furniture that broke completely with the look of its predecessor, Rococo Revival. To some extent, it expressed the industrial explosion of the times after the Civil War. A tremendous sense of optimism—a feeling that machines could make things better, that poor men could become rich—propelled many into the making of fortunes. It was the beginning of what has since been called the Gilded Age.

"Of course, there was another side, the excesses, the corruption, but I think this furniture expresses the better side of all that." So speaks this single-minded West Coast collector nonpareil, whose philosophy and sense of history come resoundingly across in a collection of Renaissance Revival furniture—over sixty pieces strong, room after room of it, bold and gleaming in the house (ca. 1886) he and his wife have restored. Side notes to the main collection are Victorian silver-plate and American brilliant-cut glass, but the furniture, striking in scale, dominant in its consistency and cohesiveness of vision, takes center stage.

Walking in and among the collection—seeing so many of these pieces grouped together—one can't help but ex-

Opposite: **The tall-ceilinged double parlor, where massive pieces of Renaissance Revival furniture are placed for maximum power and effect. In the foreground, the inlaid center table is in the Neo-Grec style. The heavily carved armchair and sidechair upholstered in a silk damask are part of a set, with a long griffin-carved sofa produced by Allen Brothers of Philadelphia.** *Above:* **The informal dining area off the kitchen, painted white, shows off the ornate Renaissance Revival furniture. On the left, the rolltop desk with its spindled gallery is typical of Grand Rapids furniture made in the early 1870s.**

perience their vigorous masculinity. This is, no question, powerful stuff, the audacious and unconditional choices of our most flamboyant robber-baron's dreams. One can feel the excitement and intensity of the century that produced these pieces and the people they were made for. That impact is only magnified by the perceptive way in which this husband and wife have chosen to present the collection. "We were authentic in our restoration of the house itself," they explain, "but not in the color, floors and window treatments. We wanted a bright house that would offset the massiveness of the furniture."

So the furniture stands alone. Walls and ceilings were painted in pale, creamy shades; windows left bare so the sunlight could stream in; floors—unstained oak and highly polished—laid over an original fir subfloor that in the 19th century would have been carpeted. It is a startling setting for such solid and elaborately carved furniture, but, somehow, a suitable backdrop. Bravado makes it work.

Like many, this collection began with simple pieces: first came the small secretary desk, now in the home office (which houses no less than eight other examples of the style). From there the obsession grew. A Christian Herter cabi-

Right: A large carved cabinet made by the firm of Robert Mitchell and Frederick Rammelsberg, Cincinnati (ca. 1870s), holds primarily large pieces of American brilliant-cut glass. Produced from the 1880s to around 1915, these distinctly American pieces are characterized by extremely elaborate, deep-cut, all-over designs, a style quite different from the European glass produced at the time. Surprisingly, there is a high survival rate among good pieces of this glass. An expensive commodity then and now, it was highly prized and therefore treated with great care.

Left: The original woodwork, wainscoting, and walls in the dining room used a pale palette to create a feeling of light. The cabinets are the original built-ins. Against the wall there is a small walnut Neo-Grec piece, from the early 1870s, with characteristic ebonized trim and incised gilt lines; above it, a 19th-century American landscape. "I've made a conscious attempt to have things in the house that are clearly American," Berke says. The period dining-room table is surrounded by eight Renaissance Revival chairs, a Victorian interpretation of a common 18th-century slatted style.

Top and above: Victorian clocks—collected for their cases, which resemble Berke's favorite furniture—stand tall in his office. *Left:* This ten-foot-high rosewood cabinet designed by Thomas Brooks in the late 1860s is carved with bird dogs, cherubs, and an unidentified gentleman, possibly the original owner. The five-point star on the interior of the desk portion suggests that this might have been a dedication piece. Next to it, an ebonized and gilded pedestal holds one of a collection of silverplate card receivers, in which visitors to 19th-century homes left their calling cards.

Above: A soup tureen with goat and deer heads and hoofed legs. When Berke began collecting, he was captivated by the whimsical qualities and mixed motifs of 19th-century silverplate, which sometimes reflected as many as five architectural styles in one sugar bowl. "The inspiration seemed to come from a thousand random sources." *Opposite:* a Victorian silverplate calling-card holder.

net in the dining room is a favorite, as is a ladies' drop-center dressing mirror upstairs. This last is a tour de force of rosewood carving—Victorian ladies, lion-head supports on candle brackets. But there are less illustrious upstarts that tickle one's collecting fancy. The side cabinet in the back parlor, with goofy gears on top, is a slap-happy tribute to the Machine Age, and probably a piece out of one of the big midwestern furniture factories of the time. "I loved it when I saw it," the collector recalls. "It struck me as being so naïve and unsophisticated."

That feeling permeates the collection of silverplate as well, which includes all sorts of pieces but especially card receivers. What stimulated the production of silverplate was the tremendous deposits of silver being mined in California, Colorado, and Nevada during the 19th century. The flood of silver, combined with the relatively new technology of electroplating, made these pieces possible. The Victorians immediately embraced the luxury of affordable silver.

Almost all Victoriana collectors tend to speak of an intangible "glow," a "feeling," or "voice" they hear when they see something they want to call their own. The owners here are no exception. While lamenting how hard it is for West Coast collectors to get first crack at many top pieces, it's obvious this has not stopped many prizes from finding a good home. And—"This house wasn't decorated" he points out. "These pieces were acquired because I loved them. There was never any question about finding a place where they all would go."

PEACOCK FEVER

Opposite: These glorious peacock-feather fans were purchased on a trip to India, where "peacocks are as common as pigeons." They're displayed on the parlor's peacock carpet, an authentic Victorian pattern inspired by the Japanese textiles of the time, which was specially commissioned for Labine's peacock room. Designed in 1877 by Benjamin Perks and reproduced by the original English mill, this would have been a fairly avant-garde carpet pattern for that time (the famous Liberty of England peacock patterns weren't created until nearly ten years later).

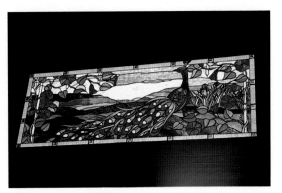

Above: A panel of stained glass designed by artist Ernest Porcelli and adapted from period designs replaced the plain glass transom in the entryway, which the Labines found too cold-looking. The house was built in 1883, a Neo-Grec–style brownstone, one of a row of ten built on speculation by an enterprising Victorian named Dorrity.

Just inside the tall walnut and walnut burl doors of Clem and Claire Labine's restored 1883 brownstone, in Brooklyn, New York, a clue, but hardly more than that, hints at what is to come. It hovers overhead: a brilliantly colored peacock-patterned stained-glass panel, inset into the transom above the doors.

Once inside, it is clear the house itself, with its soaring 13-foot ceilings, its ornamental stenciling (even the backs of the stairway treads are stenciled and discreetly ornamented) is a 19th-century-addict's dream. But the peacocks lurk everywhere. They are, literally, underfoot, in a glorious wall-to-wall peacock-feathered carpet, an authentic 1887 design the Labines commissioned especially for this room. A stuffed specimen, mounted on the wall, rules over its own parlor jungle. Peacocks appear on the brass fire screen, peacock figurines sit on the side tables, feathery peacock fans are scattered here and there. Finally, there's the pièce-de-résistance—the oversize, hand-painted frieze encircling the parlor, with the spectacular nestling peacocks forming the central medallion overhead. In creating the ceiling medallion, Christopher Dresser, the influential Victorian art critic and designer, was the "design consultant," Labine says. At the turn of the

An assemblage of Victoria and Albert commemoratives creates a parlor "shrine." On the wall, a romanticized engraving of the young Victoria at Covent Garden. The large Parian Albert is a memorial commemorative, issued on his death in 1861; a naïve painted "Albert" figurine sits near the bronze Victoria bust. On the lower level, a pressed-glass Jubilee plate and china cup along with Victoria and Albert wedding portraits; above that, a tin coronation box, a mid-century Staffordshire Victoria, and an inscribed Dalton/Lambert Jubilee jug. The ceramic pitcher is another rare commemorative of Albert's death.

Clockwise from top left: A cup and saucer set issued for the 1897 Diamond Jubilee; a rare early commemorative lozenge case celebrating the November 21, 1840, birth of Victoria and Albert's first child; a pink lusterware saucer honoring the wedding of Victoria and Albert (February 10, 1840); a china cup honoring the Diamond Jubilee; seen front and back, a tiny, rare Albert memorial tape measure; and a colorful tin that looks like a biscuit or chocolate tin but was sold to the Labines as a collar box commemorating Queen Victoria's 1837 coronation.

Above: **This vintage peacock, stuffed and wall-mounted, inhabits its own parlor jungle. The woodwork in the house is American walnut; the shutters are original.**

century, when the home's interiors were "Colonial Revivalized," the original and rather ornate rosette was ripped out and the chaste Colonial Revival circlet shown here put in its stead. Taking their lead from Dresser, who scorned dimensional plaster ornamentation in favor of stylized painted designs, they commissioned this painted peacock-inspired version in the same spreading size as the original.

Peacock fever came on several years ago when the Labines were in "the grips of the Aesthetic Movement," Clem recalls. The peacock is the well-known symbol of that style. Stuffed peacocks abounded in artistic Victorian homes; peacocks were embroidered on piano shawls and table covers; and tall vases spilled over with glistening feathers to

sound a nearly universal 19th-century theme. Claire had fallen in love with Whistler's Peacock rooms at the Frick Museum in New York, the inspiration for many a proper Victorian peacock room during the original period. Responding to the charge of extraordinary flamboyance, the Labines recall a favorite Victorian maxim: "Anything worth doing is worth doing to excess."

The wildly fantastical hand-painted frieze is far and away more elaborate than anything the original owners of the home would have commissioned. "This is a Victorian fantasy, not a historical restoration," Labine explains. In researching the house, there was just no evidence of any exciting paint schemes. What did turn up—"snippets behind the

baseboards"—he says, "were drab and mundane, the mediocre taste of the period, rather than the stuff of the period that interested me."

What also interests them are Victoria and Albert commemoratives, particularly those of Prince Albert, which are rare. "We started out buying Queen Victorias as the symbol of the era which is closest to my heart. But the more I read, the more I realized what a singular fellow Albert was." Albert's most lasting monument, Labine points out, is in fact Britain's royal family. Albert was schooled in the idea of royalty as the servant of the people and he brought that concept to the monarchy, making his own royal family a model for England."

The collection they've accumu-

The extraordinary hand-painted and gilded peacock frieze wraps the upper portion of the walls in the main parlor. Based on a French Art Nouveau design, the sprawling 3-foot-wide frieze covers an expanse of more than 50 feet and includes a matching peacock ceiling medallion. The ceiling here is glazed in an antique parchment tone; the 19th-century brass light fixture is somewhat older than the house.

lated illustrates the variety of Victorian commemorative souvenirs—tins and lozenge containers, cups and saucers, jugs, pitchers, prints, even an Albert memorial tape measure. Commemoratives honoring Victoria's reign from 1837 to 1887, and her Diamond Jubilee ten years later may be easier to come by, but early commemoratives from the 1840s—Victoria and Albert wedding items or a commemorative honoring the birth of their first child— all issued before the real passion for such souvenirs exploded, are quite rare. The impetus for the collection, however, says Labine, is not the value of the objects, but the personal and emotional associations. As the pottery jug sentimentally says of Queen Victoria: "She Brought Her People Lasting Good."

7

THEMATIC **INTERPRETATIONS**

Some collectors of 19th-century treasures find that the house itself, its rooms and contents, comprise the sum and scope of their collection. In these cases, the "collection" flows from room to room as a mix, in a personal interpretation, with no particular concentration on any single type

STEINWAY

NORWICH

"WAUREGAN HOUSE"

December 15th, 1892.

CENTENNIAL
CELEBRATION
1789 — 1889
EMPLOYEES
STEINWAY
& SONS

HOSE C
NO. 3

39th Annual
B. F.
BINGHAMTON
AUG. 30, 18

of object. While individual collections of Victoriana may, of course, be included within the whole, the effect is that of a complete environment, sometimes whimsical, always personal, with a rich variety of otherwise unrelated objects, their Victorian pedigree being their common bond.

More than any other category, this type of collection depends on the collector's personal vision, whether impulsive or instinctive. It can take the form of a thick tangle of tassels and cords, in old gold, crimson, blue, and green, clustered on a column as a play on Victorian ornament. Or, a mantelscape of pinecones, greenery and propped-up photo portraits —partly a salute to the Victorian love of nature, but also a bow to its charm.

The collectors here collect all sorts of 19th-century objects, things they find intriguing, aesthetically pleasing, things that touch in them some inner chord—the appeal of their design, by the associations they suggest. Often, there's some imaginative bit of period-play in a collection like this; or, the collection might reveal a playful side—an almost frolicsome sense of accumulation that doesn't take itself too seriously. On occasion, the mix might include pieces from other periods; it depends.

Mostly, though, the house-as-a-collection concept is the collector's individual perception of some particular aspect of the 19th-century sensibility. Done well, it's collecting that's expansive, all-encompassing, and spontaneous, well suited to the nature of Victoriana.

GENTLEMAN JIM

Jim Rogers is just such an interpretive collector. While he did not exactly set out to collect Victoriana, he says, he collected what he liked. "What I liked just happened to be Victorian." His five-story American Renaissance townhouse (ca. 1899–1900), now restored, was also an impetus. Wanting to remain true to the flavor of the house somehow worked together with collecting what he liked. The result: a combination of furnishings, idiosyncratic personal collectibles, and sporting memorabilia that is Rogers's answer to his fantasy of living in a turn-of-the-century men's club.

Rogers's vision was the sort of welcoming, unfussy, undecorated elegance one might have found in a traditional British club during the closing years of the century and, perhaps, the following "Edwardian" decade. Steadfast Victorian decorative themes were used to match the tone. The original mahogany paneling was restored after several years of painstaking paint stripping (before Rogers bought it, the house was being used as a Jesuit dormitory); patterned wallpapers and ornate borders imparted a sense of luxury; properly well-worn layered rugs added the patina of tradition. The furniture may include pieces from other periods, but strong-looking Victorian pieces set the tone: 19th-century leather chairs, a Pugin center table, a carved Renaissance Revival bed, tables and windows veiled with frosty Edwardian lace. In essence, it's a multigenerational Victorian mix.

Enlisting the aid of decorator Keith Irvine on his quest for the tone of a "gentlemen's club," Rogers incorporated his favorite objects and collectibles into the rooms—paraphernalia acquired on motorcycle jaunts through the Yukon, China, and Thailand (for a look at the exotic streak running through his collection, see pages 140 to 143); early-century crew memorabilia and sailing mementos; framed Confederate currency and old-time treasury bills (Rogers collects what he jokingly calls "worthless money"—of value only to the collector). The effect as a whole is a "Hail fellow, well met" cheer that re-creates the casual but elegant comfort, the clubby jumble, that Rogers envisioned from the outset.

Opposite: **The sitting area, with original leaded glass windows, created out of what was technically known as the square stair landing, is one of the most comfortable areas of the house. The wraparound window seat, piled high with 19th-century needlework pillows, recalls a Victorian cozy corner. The marble bust and needlepoint footstool are both 19th century.** *Left:* **A Currier & Ives print, *The Bachelor,* hangs over the entryway fireplace.**

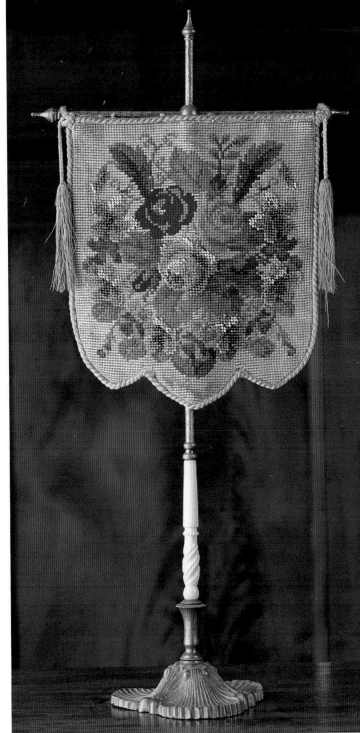

Left: A grand view of the main floor. On the drawing-room sofa, a spectacular crimson Victorian beadwork cushion of calla lilies. Beyond that, the landing with sitting area acts as a transitional space from the warm, drawing-room tones to the dark splendor of the traditional banquet hall, paneled in oak, with beamed ceiling, bronze chandelier, and a massive Renaissance Revival dining table and chairs. *Right:* On the drawing-room mantel (and against the restored mahogany paneling), an unusual tasseled candle screen, also called a lamp screen, was used to shield the candle glow from drafts. *Household Elegancies,* written in 1875, points out that these screens could also be useful in a sickroom or nursery to shade the crib or a sleeping baby.

Opposite: The "green room" (once a billiard room) includes a handsome late-century English scrap screen. The mottled green walls are covered with prints, sailing memorabilia, framed currency, and personal mementos. *Left:* Special details add to the ambience—19th-century brass sconces with etched-glass globes, a Victorian barometer on the drawing-room wall. Also in the drawing room, vintage lace ornamented with fringe and crystals and a collection of Victorian needlework pillows. Irvine first introduced these to Rogers, who has since continued to collect: "As you can see, I accepted them wholeheartedly." *Above:* An old-fashioned 19th-century rolltop desk littered with favorite photos and assorted small collectibles is the focal point of a study. *Overleaf:* Light streams in through vintage leaded-glass windows over a cozy corner.

"Vienna Moire"
THE POPULAR DESK BLOTTER

A Large Assortment of Colors

STATIONERY STORE COMPLETE WITH

MADE ONLY BY
Albemarle Paper
RICHMOND, VIRGINIA

Object Lessons

Personal mementos and collections warm the lean lines of the loft, beginning with the brick-walled entry, *above.* On the desk, *opposite,* are objects masquerading as something else, a device the Victorians delighted in; the miniature desk is really a bank, the camera is a candy container. The "pinwheels" are a 19th-century fortune-telling game. *Top right:* more collectibles—dice and old-fashioned game counters. *Right:* part of the hand collection—the frozen-in-time "movement" of mannequin hands, artist's models, Victorian ring holders, and glove molds. The small, open porcelain hand in the foreground is reputed to be a model from one of Queen Victoria's children.

Stepping into this collector's loft is like stepping into a storybook scene of Victorian childhood. A forest of eerie, enchanted images—babies, toys, dolls, clowns, and animals—gives a first impression of innocence but then a disquieting edge. It's almost as if one were entangled in the turnabout magic of one of Grimm's fairy tales.

This sensibility shows itself in the deliberate, ofttimes provocative placement of seemingly unrelated objects into the fantasy still lifes and arresting tabletop vignettes that fill the space. Here, the collections are the thing, ever so gently, but ever so deliberately taking us in hand. There are Victorian smalls of all kinds—alphabet pieces, buttons, tiny toys, miniatures—along with dolls, mannequin hands, and grinning clowns. Boxes are stacked almost ceiling high with collected objects. The Victorian fascination with home taxidermy is expressed here too. Woodland animals, birds, puppies, and baby lion cubs watching and peeking, are the real scene-stealers.

"My mother was a collector so I grew up with it," explains the owner, a professional photographer who shares the loft with her husband. "She never threw anything away, not even flyers from the grocery store." To this day, in fact, she

Above: The main table in the loft offers a dramatic tabletop still life. From left to right are an ornate 19th-century European sewing box; commemorative Victorian ribbons and badges; tasseled ribbons from lodge events and memoriams; papier-mâché piglets (the sleeping one is a candy container); tiny stuffed baby pups (Micro and Scopic) set in adult positions; pieces of vintage games (dice, old-fashioned game counters, and pickup sticks in a cylindrical black holder). The Victorian mourning vignette includes a salesman's sample, train tickets, and baby photos (ca. 1879).

Left: Visual proof that the wide-open space of a loft can be intimate and inviting. Collections and vignettes create boundaries instead of walls, bringing the tall-windowed space down to earth. *Opposite:* A niche was created over the doorway to the bedroom for this happy group—an old terra-cotta baby's head, forest creatures dressed in heavy crimson tassels, and delicate 19th-century Parisian baby dresses.

Left: A small, unused wall in the hallway was reclaimed by carving out a glass-doored cabinet for stray smalls. *Above:* A slender table holds a collection of boxes (inside, old-fashioned teaching alphabet pieces in ivory and bone, some tinted, some plain). "I love things that come in little boxes, things you can hold cupped in the palm of your hand, like a child holding a butterfly. It comes from being a collector as a child. I was a saver, which is why I like little boxes," the owner says. The "suffragettes" are dressmaker's dolls (ca. 1910–1915). A Shaker baby chair and toy chair hold an old-fashioned painted roly-poly and other toys.

feels a special affinity for those objects that are family pieces—a terra-cotta angel or a little desk that belonged to her mother, a grandfather's musical humidor. "These are precious pieces of personal history to me," she qualifies. "There are the things I buy because I love them, but these are what I feel tender about, things that have a family history, that my mother handled and loved."

Most of the objects here have their roots in the 19th century. "I like to live with all their wonderful, whimsical expressions," she says. Yet objects with a Victorian sensibility have the power to provoke strong reactions. Often the objects she collects carry meanings beyond what they are: the chipped porcelain of a doll's head, giving it its own sense of history; a mourning vignette reminds us of the cycle of life and death that was a constant part of 19th-century daily life. As such, the collection teeters, wavering,

Left: Because it is usually so predictable in decor, a bathroom is the ideal place for a collecting display. Here, old photographs, antique dolls (a Victorian milliner's model, a folk-art couple), 19th-century baby's dresses, and other objects are especially appreciated.

Above: The toy animals in the "post office," in paper, tin, plush, and cloth, date from about 1880 to 1930. On the chest below is a two-room German dollhouse of lithographed paper on wood (ca. 1890–1910), plus assorted smalls: A soft-metal Victorian carriage, tussie-mussie holders, antique dance cards, and an albino raccoon and friend.

wobbling along the thin, thin line between the joyful and the macabre.

The collections of 19th-century taxidermy bring the natural world into the interior. "The Victorians collected nature—whether it was sea mosses, birds, animals, or shells. For them, it was a marriage of the internal and external worlds." As with pressed flowers, it was their way of preserving natural beauty. Today, the presence of well-loved animals and birds adds a sense of comfort and peace to the home, a contrast to the "concrete jungle" of today's world.

Collecting is an active, organic process, and the objects here are in a constant state of change, moving from surface to surface throughout the space. "Buy something because you like it, not because it looks great beside the couch," the owner suggests. "It can move." In her home, a grouping might be on a tabletop one day, another day, somewhere else entirely. "It depends what I am working on. If I'm thinking about dance cards, they're displayed in various places. If the subject is babies, they're around."

Top: Familiar associations with objects are turned upside down in a curiously tantalizing vignette of unrelated items: an 18th-century polychrome Baby Jesus, a Victorian shadow box of stuffed birds, an heirloom silverplate candlestick, a 19th-century leather photo album, a gilded angel, and mannequin hands.

Above: On the dining table, a "peaceable kingdom"—a small grouping of lion cubs tied with baby-pink ribbons. *Left:* toys in the kitchen—tins, paper soldiers, celluloids, clowns, rolypolys. The clown heads are actually candy containers.

Opposite: In most of these groupings, scale is disregarded. "I just juxtapose things," the collector says. On the kitchen counter, a spectacular Victorian bell jar holds an assortment of birds, including hummingbirds. These were a familiar sight in the mid-19th-century parlor, where, in addition to stuffed birds, a bell jar might house an intricate arrangement of shell or bead flowers, wax fruit, or other treasured and interesting objects the Victorians wished to highlight and protect.

An Ornamental Aesthetic

With its elaborate 19th-century wallpapers and decorative ceiling treatments, its opulent Renaissance Revival and Aesthetic-era furnishings, the Alameda home of this West Coast couple might strike the uninitiated at first as a period-perfect recreation. On further glance, it is clear that the collectors have a more personal view of the Victorian spirit, with several strongly defined collections within the home. Their collection is inspired as much by a driving interest in the aesthetics of Victorian design as by the 1890 roots of the house itself. "We don't see ourselves as period collectors," they say. "While we want to evoke the context of the time, we've never done it with any conscious attempt at period accuracy."

Instead, what they have collected during the course of their marriage are objects and antiques they have responded to instinctively. Initially drawn into Victoriana by the woodwork and the parquet floors, as well as the gables, turrets, and porches of their Queen Anne home, their sensibilities have since been wooed by the ornamental aesthetic of certain 19th-century objects. The stylized lines of ebonized furniture from the 1870s, the gilded drama of High Renaissance Revival pieces, the exquisite decorative bindings of choice vintage books, even their late-

As they collected, the couple found they preferred unusual examples of Victorian silverplate, particularly those with Aesthetic, animal, or Renaissance motifs.

century Anglo-Japanese transfer-printed china—all were collected independently, yet all exhibit a common thread—the couple's predilection for the ornamental, very graphic design themes of the 1870s. One of the more unusual pieces in the couple's collection is their prized Pairpoint silverplate lamp, which, with its bird and animal motifs, also picks up on the stylized designs that both collectors admire.

Their taste could be said to be surprisingly ornate for an admittedly modern professional couple, yet they feel perfectly at home with elaborate designs. A subtle counterbalance in decoration makes it all easy to live with. While the arrangement of the parlor furniture, for example, reflects an authentic 19th-century mode, the elimination of drapery on the windows, on the tables, plus the lack of clutter, is a decidedly 20th-century taste.

The couple's taste for Victoriana was realized slowly over a number of

Left: Among the albums on the parlor center table is one that includes not only a complete set of family portraits but also an intricate Victorian family tree and photographs of the home's interiors. The bound collection of *St. Nicholas* volumes, the popular Victorian children's magazine, is another find. Published from the 1870s through the 1920s, bound volumes such as these were often presented as Christmas gifts to young children.

years, beginning first with a natural attraction to the stylized, linear gilding on great pedimented Renaissance Revival pieces and the quirky delicacy of the flying fans and birds and Aesthetic doodads popping off Anglo-Japanese plates and pitchers and platters. It was further heightened by research into the origins of what they had acquired. A new collection —the architectural and Victorian design books in the back-parlor library—is the result of just some of the research they've done on each piece.

The unusual seven-piece parlor set by John Jelliff, a prominent Newark cabinetmaker during the 1860s and 1870s, known for superb rosewood furniture adorned with carved ladies' heads and bronze or brass medallions cresting the backs of chairs and settees, is but one example of their painstaking research. They discovered that the motifs on their pieces matched those on a set owned by Jelliff's own daughter, currently in the collection at the Newark Museum. The inlay on the skirts of the chairs was identical. In another effort, a thorough inspection of the carved walnut dining-room sideboard turned up a label and paperwork—in French.

As newlyweds, in their early collecting days, the two discovered they occasionally had different likes and dislikes. Since then, however, their tastes have evolved in the same sure way, as their educated eyes hone in, almost instinctively these days, on the same things. The result: a unique and very defined joint collection.

Above: The gilded ornamental bindings of this collection of Victorian poetry books, chosen for subject and for appearance and all from the 1880s, can be seen through the glass doors of a small ebonized cabinet. *Right and opposite:* A massive Wooten patent desk, officially called a Queen Anne Pattern Cabinet Secretary, signed by desk trimmer Zue Jackson and dated March 14, 1889, proves a wonderful way to display collectibles and still keep them accessible. Here, ephemera of all kinds—trade and calling cards, postcards, prints, and maps—spills from the nooks and cubbies.

8

PERIOD-**P**ERFECT **C**OLLECTING

Collectors who go "period-perfect"—creating authentic "time-tunnel" interiors as settings for their collections— are a special breed. They have the discipline of the single-minded collector, but with a special focus. Theirs is the ability to hone in on a particular period and the fortitude

not to be swayed from a historic sphere, no matter how attractive the temptation. The visual reward is of the most unique and satisfying sort—one owns a time capsule: the 19th-century objects are so fully in tune with their surroundings that it takes only the smallest bit of imagination to transcend time barriers.

The re-creation of period interiors, of course, is an intensely Victorian pastime. Americans in 1876 fell in love with American history and began to re-create Colonial furnishings and artifacts, right down to pseudo spinning wheels and butter churns, which, it was felt, most properly evoked the era. These earnest Victorian efforts at historicism spurred what is now called Colonial Revival—an expression of the Victorians' romanticized view of 18th-century domestic life. Victorians' newly awakened reverence for historical allusion was too often at odds with their natural inclination toward industry and progress.

Of course, any period interior has to be seen in light of the prejudices and scholarship of the era of revival. Victorians' Colonial interiors are more Victorian than Colonial, just as their Anglo-Japanese efforts were decidedly Anglo as opposed to Japanese. Not so though, with the following collectors' attempts. A wisp of 20th-century sensibility may slip in here and there, but for the most part, the taste and tradition of the last century is the dominant decorative influence in the two homes displayed in this chapter.

Many people today are intrigued with creating period-perfect Victorian settings. The two collector pairs highlighted here, however, have approached that goal in far from the usual ways. The first, using the magnificent setting of a southern home (ca. 1883) as the base for a rich bastion of regionally oriented, multigenerational collecting; the second, pursuing period-perfect collecting as 19th-century immigrants might have collected. Truly disciplined—and truly fascinating—collectors and collections all.

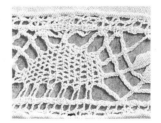

SOUTHERN COMFORT

Above: A collection of Minton Anglo-Japanese china adorns a bedroom table. *Opposite:* The wide central hall allows the Millers to display an excellent collection of 19th-century paintings and is the result of the house's being built on a symmetrical Greek Revival plan, with large, 20 by 20-foot rooms branching off on either side. The woodwork is black walnut and butternut, with black walnut floors; the restored stenciling is original to the house.

One feels the "period" mood the moment one drives up to Marcie and Richard Miller's Victorian home, built about 1883. Outside, near the curb, a flickering, gaslit streetlamp, the only one left in this tiny Georgia town, and an old-fashioned carriage stoop mark their home as special. Once inside, the feeling is nothing short of a romantic trip back to the splendors of the 19th century: warm and inviting as only southern homes can be, comfortable, familial—in short, the 19th century of affectionate memory, less the residual stiffness or primness of the era. While the Miller interpretation is romanticized, it resounds with authenticity and the elegance of the period.

The house, which was built as a showcase for a prominent local judge and his "amiable and accomplished wife," was originally decorated and furnished by local craftsmen and artists. When the Millers purchased it in 1978—"We looked up at the parlor ceiling and immediately said we would take it"—the handiwork that had so impressed Victorian townfolk nearly a hundred years earlier was still pristine—"aesthetically untouched," the Millers recall. Considering that the woodwork had never been repainted and the house had never been divided (which meant its original layout remained in-

A spectacular painted ceiling sets the tone in the parlor. The furniture is very much what one might have found in a well-to-do multigenerational southern home of the time. The piano (ca. 1887) was ordered by the original owners especially for the house. The drop-leaf mahogany Empire table and silk-upholstered chairs are from the 1840s. The étagère (ca. 1855) is a typical New Orleans piece. The placement of the New England highboy (ca. 1790) in the parlor reflects the Victorian practice of keeping a family's finest pieces in the front of the house, although traditionally, highboys wouldn't have been found in Victorian homes. In this context, though, it reflects the Colonial Revival style of the last quarter of the 19th century, as well as generational roots.

tact), the structural problems seemed minor. Too, the last modernization was in 1916, when electricity and plumbing were brought in, which meant these major hurdles were covered.

Even more fortuitous, an enviable amount of original furniture—a Renaissance Revival bed in the master bedroom, a Prudent Mallard armoire, several rockers, the piano, Gothic Revival hall chairs, and other artifacts—remained and was sold along with the house. The Millers aimed to restore the house to its bygone splendor and revive it to showcase the furnishings inside.

The grandeur of the home's wide, central hallway, repainted a rosy crimson and embellished with elaborate stencilwork, is now impeccably restored. Upon entering, one passes the 9-foot high grandfather's clock on the landing, Empire pier tables filled with clustered glass-domed bell jars, small art objects, marble busts. The unusual width of the hallway accommodates a collection of 19th-century oils ("It was Richard who saw the need for oil paintings and began the collection," Marcie Miller says), a feature the narrower halls of city town houses and other 19th-century buildings would not allow.

Before the Millers began collecting they plunged into research. Originally steered toward Eastlake-style pieces, they soon realized that these were hardly appropriate to the house (described in 1883 as "one of the most beautiful and costly residences ever built in this city." "We need to look for things with paws," was the way Richard Miller put it.

They also found the region as well as the period affected their collections, with an affinity for southern regional furnishings emerging. The home's upstairs houses a collection of southern primitive pieces. The course of the extensive research even forged a new career for Marcie Miller, who has since founded a historical research library to aid homeowners, designers, and architects on the long road to period-perfect Victorian style.

The Millers wanted to re-create a multigenerational family feeling in their home. Although the heart of the decor reflects the opulence of the 1880s, pieces from earlier periods are also used, as these would have been passed down from generation to generation. Such a treatment would keep the rooms from becoming static and avoid the artifical "museum-y" feeling one so often experiences in period rooms. Accordingly, although Renaissance Revival furnishings represent the latest strain of collecting, Rococo Revival (typical of New Orleans), Empire, and Gothic Revival furnishings; a circular Meeks center table; and even a splendid late 18th-century New England highboy contribute to the dynamic collection. The result is a Victorian eclecticism with a somewhat finer, more traditional feeling than most. Enhancing the displays are various pieces of vintage clothing—gloves, a pair of eyeglasses, a fan, and other objects from Marcie Miller's collection. A piece of lace, some needlework, and a bedcover all add a sense of life and reflect the period as it was in its heyday.

Opposite top: The hand-stenciled ceiling features a southern regional theme mixed with classical motifs—urns, vines, and flowers. All of the greenery shown can be found on the Millers' property. *Center:* Collectibles include antique books and an old-fashioned decanter. The Millers received the needlepoint/petit-point fan, shaped like a miniature fire screen, as a wedding present. *Bottom:* In furnishing the bedroom the Millers chose objects that were typically southern. Many of the pieces they found, from homes in the area, have a similar feel, as if they were all ordered from the same manufacturer. The Renaissance Revival walnut bed and small wicker rocker are original to this room; the antique pillow shams and bedcover are crimson silk satin and tatting. At the foot of the bed stands an Empire table with matching side chairs (ca. 1840–1850).

Left: During the 19th century, a piano in the parlor indicated an interest in culture and the arts. This ebonized piano (ca. 1887; specially ordered from New York), with unusual decorative panels and its companion mantelpiece, were symbols of wealth during the 1880s. The cranberry velvet inset, also featured on the piano stool and the mantel, was an opulent customized touch that would have impressed visitors at the time.

Left: Sewing/needlework and personal items are common objects that one would have found in an old-time bedroom; on the bedside table here are an old-fashioned sewing basket filled with wooden darning eggs and vintage sewing implements, an antique fan, and gloves. *Bottom left:* Marcie Miller displays some of her vintage clothing collection—here a rust-colored traveling suit and lace shawl—on a Victorian dressmaker's form. The white satin shoes belonged to Aunt Sarah, a relative of the original owners, who occupied the house from about 1910 to 1930. The period collage on the wall is made of scrap images of 19th-century children and animals; below it, a framed Victorian lace baby dress. *Opposite:* The Millers' collection of Victorian silver and silverplate, on display in the dining room, includes this elegant castor set, a staple on Victorian dinner tables everywhere.

PARLOR GAMES

John Raymond and Philip Rudko have created an unusually complex and intellectual variation on the period-perfect theme. Not content with arranging their extensive collection in a merely authentic way, they chose to re-create the manner in which their 19th-century immigrant ancestors might have approached their New World environments. Accordingly, Rudko, of Russian Orthodox background, assembled a collection of Victoriana heavily laced with 19-century Russian and French artifacts ("French items were emulated in the Russian Empire," he points out). The heritage of Raymond's parents —French and Irish, made even more complicated by a strong tie to the pre–Civil War South—influenced his collections in turn. For both, the immigrant theme seemed not only challenging but historically appropriate. "There were so many people leaving Europe and moving to the United States at the turn of the century that it seemed worthwhile to explore," Rudko explains.

An overview of these interiors, housed in a turn-of-the-century flat, reveals several layers of collecting. The collection starts with the sort of objects immigrants might have brought with them from the old country, interspersed with furniture reflecting middle-class taste but

Opposite: Through an arch of Victorian fretwork and draped vintage portieres, the front parlor appears much as it would have a century ago, with furniture that is respectable but far from high style. The seven-piece Renaissance Revival parlor set would have been fashionable in the 1870s but is appropriately and intentionally reupholstered in a later fabric. *Below:* The 19th-century French mantel clock and accessories reflect Raymond's French-Irish heritage. The center table is draped with a covering from the collectors' extensive collection of vintage fabrics. The Colonial Revival mantel, with original tilework, dates from 1897.

of somewhat lower economic status. The design of the door glass in one bedroom, for example, was copied from a period illustration and selected because it would have been accessible during the late 19th century, neither a particularly expensive nor an intricate design. In the parlor, they tried to re-create a typical middle-class American room, using furniture, accessories, and textiles in a manner that was a bit dated, which wasn't uncommon in the period.

Closer scouting reveals an awareness of the kind of fads that would have tickled the fancy of the Victorian middle class, especially the penchant for souvenirs of all kinds. Within the collection is another collection: the old-time Edison phonographs—five in all—that crop up in various rooms throughout the house. This diverges from a period-perfect theme: in the 19th-century there would only have been one per family. Although we see the nostalgic charm of these machines today, the Victorians thought them ugly and hid them away, bringing them out only to entertain guests. The one with the floral painted horn was probably an attempt to make what the Victorians found a fascinating but unattractive device somewhat more aesthetically palatable.

One bedroom is furnished in the Aesthetic style, with Japanesque accessories and accents, chosen in the way a French-Irish Catholic immigrant, either one generation removed or fresh off the boat, might have perceived that artistic style, picking up on Aestheticism somewhat after its heyday, often in a charm-

Above: **This old-time oak telephone (ca. 1907) was rewired with modern workings.** *Opposite:* **A narrow hallway table with a collection of daguerreotypes, tintypes (which replaced the former in popularity during the 1860s), and other vintage photographs, including ones of John Raymond's Civil War ancestors, emphasizes the interest in family heritage. The hallway itself is lined with more family portraits, framed prints, and art.**

Above: **An Aesthetic-style bedroom reflects the interpretation of a turn-of-the-century French immigrant of modest means. The oak country French bed dates from 1870. The marble-topped commode (ca. 1878) is draped to conceal what the Victorians would have felt was the cold, bare look of white marble.**
Left: **A Japanese fan and prints provide proper Aesthetic touches in this cozy bedroom corner. The reclining patent rocker dates from 1893; the mirror is Anglo-Japanese. The late-19th-century machine-woven textile on the table was made to imitate the fine silk weaving of more costly materials.**

ingly naïve way. In that room, a visitor would immediately notice a wallscape including several devotional icons: a turn-of-the-century "bleeding heart" as well as an altar piece (ca. 1877). Their placement in the bedroom reflects the historical complexity behind this particular collection. "Although many Catholics came to this country during the last quarter of the 19th century, Catholicism was still considered an alien religion," Raymond says. While it might have been acceptable to hire a Catholic, it would have been necessary for such an immigrant to keep his religious art and shrines in a personal place, the bedroom, out of public view.

Objects in the two bedrooms reflect further distinctions in this unique variation on period-perfect collecting. The Russian-style bedroom reflects the Victorian taste for the exotic in particularly subtle ways: even the simple table coverings are embroidered; the handiwork items, such as the tinsel art, and the needlepoint bellpull, are colorful, detailed and ornate, in contrast to the subdued colors of the Aesthetic bedroom, which contains collections of a utilitarian nature —the sewing machine and threads. A Victorian collector with an Aesthetic bent might be expected to have a taste for homespun crafts (as exhibited in the display of American Indian beadwork) as opposed to fancywork.

The decorative philosophy behind the period-perfect parlor is particularly intricate. In researching the parlor set, the collectors determined it was from Grand Rapids, the great midwestern furniture center of the 19th century, and was

Below: An elaborate, tasseled lambrequin drapes the Eastlake-style mantel in the Russian bedroom. Here, objects that would have been brought over from the old country reflect a French-Russian 19th-century flavor. Porcelains, turquoise glass vases, and the glittering bronze clock are all French (ca. 1870–1880). The clock, a copy of a finer version, would have been a typically middle-class Victorian acquisition of the time. The elegant beadwork mantel adornments date from around 1880. The period table cover is an embroidered chenille; the pillow, a gift from a family member, is Russian and dates from the turn of the century.

Above: This marble-topped dresser showcases an assortment of Victoriana, including an exquisite late-19th-century gilded French porcelain basin and pitcher, a Victorian hat ornament (a lesser bird of paradise in its original box), and a beaded collar box still filled with collars. The Russian pocketwatch is from 1855.

Above: The Aesthetic-style bedroom is the setting for this graceful Edison Triumph D (1910) and collection of vintage cylinders (in the background, a glimpse of some of the room's original woodwork: lace-draped cabinet doors). The custom-ordered oak horn was an attempt to upgrade the appearance of these musical devices.

Above: This crimson-horned Edison phonograph (ca. 1897) rests on a carved mahogany commode. The elegant Eastlake-style ebonized frames to the left hold vintage portraits. Behind the horn, a photographic mirror (ca. 1873), one of a pair, depicts *Evening.* The mahogany bed (ca. 1860) is French; the bedcover dates from the turn of the century. *Opposite:* The design of this decorative painted horn (ca. 1897) was meant to amplify the sound of the machine. A luxury item, the horn cost about $2.50, a goodly sum at the time.

probably ordered through a catalogue, as it matches photographs that mention identical "special features" available from a catalogue house at the time. The period of the upholstery, though, is not quite the same as that of the parlor set. This was deliberate on the part of Raymond and Rudko. The very convention of a parlor set would have been slightly out of date, they point out, by the closing years of the century, when unmatched pieces were considered more fashionable. An immigrant family would likely have purchased such a grouping secondhand and recovered it. While the set is indicative of middle-class taste of the 1870s, the style of the upholstery reflects a later date.

Raymond and Rudko became interested in collecting Victoriana that represented this specific middle-class taste partly out of an affinity for the objects of the 19th century, partly because the architecture of the turn-of-the-century brownstone rowhouse that houses the apartment warranted it. Not being grand, it's very much the type of home an immigrant family would have lived in at the time. Except for the placement of the bedrooms (one bedroom located at the rear of the flat was once the dining room; the other, centrally located, was once two small rooms, probably a small parlor and sitting room), most of the rooms have not been altered.

Through this very creative restoration, the passionate spirit of the collectors shows through. Explains Rudko, "When you see something that is affordable, available, and beautifully made, it demands to be taken home."

The "Kennel News" Picture Post Cards—Series 1.

whatever.

MR. PUG

fishing for wo

III

VICTORIANA DIRECTORY

Directory

Collectors turn to a variety of sources for their 19th-century treasures: many frequent auction houses and estate sales; others are regulars at flea markets, fairs, and antiques shows—big and small; still others manage, even today, to turn up worthwhile and intriguing objects at the occasional garage sale or old house sales, to come up with the fortuitous—not to say envied—attic find. The life's blood of collecting, though, comes from the dealers—those individuals who scour the country for the first tier of collectible objects and furnishings.

The dealers listed here represent a sampling of specialists in American Victoriana—sources to turn to (at a variety of price ranges) for just the sort of "cherished objects" you've seen on the preceding pages: 19th-century furniture and furnishings; textiles such as quilts, lace, and needlework; china and ceramics; silver and silverplate; glassware; vintage clothing; Victorian decorative arts and accessories; architectural antiques and more. Here and there, you will also find a listing relating to special accessories—herbal wreaths, pomanders and such—done with a special Victorian flair—items I just can't resist. While many dealers besides those listed here may include American Victoriana in their stock of objects from other times and places, an effort has been made here to list only those dealers who specialize in Victoriana or who feature it to a large extent. Enjoy your hunting for cherished objects!

A

MARJORIE PARROTT ADAMS— ANTIQUARIAN BOOKS, PRINTS & EPHEMERA
Box 117
Medway, MA 03053
(508) 533-5677

Specialty areas include the decorative arts, cookery, fashion, textiles, gardening as well as decorative bindings and Victorian color printing. Also, pressed botanical specimens, original watercolor needlework designs, and Royal Family memorabilia available.

MARK & MARJORIE ALLEN
29 Marsh Hill Road
Putnam Valley, NY 10579
(914) 528-8989

Nineteenth-century garden furnishings. Broad selection of antique cast-iron urns, fountains, seating, and tables. By appointment only.

FRANCES ALTMAN
1935 Peachtree Road, NE
Atlanta, GA 30309
(404) 355-8572

Mid- and late-Victorian linens for the bedroom and dining room. Both American and Continental examples of vintage linens.

THE ANDERSON GALLERY
21 Davis Street
Keene, NH 03431
(603) 352-6422

American and mid- and late-Victorian silver and silverplate, including tea services and large trays. Mid and late-Continental linens of fine quality, including some unusual shapes and sizes. By appointment.

ANTIQUARIAN TRADERS
8483 Melrose Avenue
Los Angeles, CA 90069
(213) 658-6394

American mid- and late-Victorian furniture, accessories, and decorative arts. Specializing in museum-quality pieces by such designers as Marcotte, Jelliff, Herter, and Berkey and Gay. Large collection of Wooten desks and other office furnishings. Restoration services available for customers.

ANTIQUE AMERICANA
146 Briddle Trail
Fairfield, CT 06430
(203) 259-5353

American mid- to late-Victorian high-quality advertising signs and tins, painted furniture, quilts, folk art, vintage coin-operated machines, advertising ephemera, with a specialty in advertising and interiors from country stores, ice-cream parlors, saloons, barbershops, and drugstores. By appointment only.

THE ANTIQUE ROOM
416 Atlantic Avenue
Brooklyn, NY 11217
(718) 875-7084

High-style American 19th-century furniture, accessories, and lighting. Furniture specialists in Greek Revival, Gothic Revival, Rococo Revival, and Renaissance Revival. Some Aesthetic Movement furniture.

APROPO
316 North Milwaukee Street
Milwaukee, WI 53202
(414) 272-5311

Furniture from all decades of the American Victorian era. Selection available in all price ranges. Some decorative arts and vintage jewelry.

ARCHITECTURAL
ANTIQUES EXCHANGE
715 North Second Street
Philadelphia, PA 19123
(215) 922-3669

Furniture from all periods of the Victorian era, lighting, antique hardware, and advertising memorabilia. Will custom-build upon request. Restoration services offered.

ARTHUR-GRAHAM, INC.
7118 North Western Avenue
Oklahoma City, OK 73116
(405) 843-4431

Late-Victorian furnishings, country furniture, and accessories. Wide range of prices.

ATTIC TREASURES
58 Ethan Allen Highway, Route 7
Ridgefield, CT 06877
(203) 544-8159

Antiques and decorative accessories from the 19th century.

B _____

BACK PORCH ANTIQUES
83 Messinger Street
St. Albans, VT 05478
(802) 524-5333

Victorian art glass, china, lamps from 1840 to 1900. Includes amberina, cranberry, sandwich glass. China includes flow-blue and Limoges.

ELIZABETH BAIRD
256 Vaughn Street
Portland, ME 04102
(207) 761-1882

Valentines, books, ephemera, and prints of exceptional quality from the 19th century. Unusual items such as hairwork, commemorative programs, greeting cards, and menus also available. By appointment only.

R. BEAUCHAMP ANTIQUES, INC.
16405 Westfield Boulevard Road
Westfield, IN 46074
(317) 621-2454

Victorian furniture and accessories mostly mid- to late-Victorian. Also, country antiques from the 19th century.

JOAN BOGART
1392 Old Northern Boulevard
Roslyn, NY 11576
(516) 621-2454

High-style American Victorian furniture, especially Belter. Large collection of American gas chandeliers with authentic shades and accessories. Appointments advisable.

BRASS LIGHT GALLERY
719 South Fifth Street
Milwaukee, WI 53204
(414) 383-0675

American mid- to late-Victorian lighting, including chandeliers, wall sconces, etc.—original and fully restored. Also carries a small line of reproduction lighting of the Victorian era.

BRATTLE BOOKSHOP
9 West Street
Boston, MA 02111
(617) 542-0210

Books and such items as parasols, ephemera, and antique pens, from the Victorian decades.

BRILLIANT ANTIQUES
8107 Maryland Avenue
St. Louis, MO 63105
(314) 725-2526

Decorative accessories (ca. 1860–1880), including brass, copper, silver, scent bottles, majolica, porcelain figures, candlesticks, and engravings.

THE BRITISH TREASURE SHOP, LTD.
P.O. Box 248
Short Hills, NJ 07078-0248
(800) 765-3500; (212) 757-7559

A wide range of 19th-century sterling silver dressing table accessories, mirrors, picture frames, ornate sterling spoons and tableware, and other small items. Specializing in antique perfume bottles and Victorian accessories with cherub motifs. A select collection of hand-crafted and signed reproductions also available. By mail or by appointment.

R. BROOKE, LTD.
960 Lexington Avenue
New York, NY 10021
(212) 535-0707

Furniture, silver, decorative antiques, and accessories of all kinds, mostly from the Victorian and Edwardian periods. Decorating services available in Victorian style.

BROOKLINE VILLAGE ANTIQUES
18 Harvard Street
Brookline, MA 02146
(617) 734-6071

Specialty includes Victorian brass chandeliers and some late-Victorian furniture and paintings. All lighting is rewired and restored.

THE BURMESE CRUET
Box 432
Montgomeryville, PA 18936
(215) 855-5388

Mail-order sales only. Specialty is American art glass from 1880 to 1910. Some English glass is also available.

C _____

CALDERWOOD GALLERY
221 South 17th Street
Philadelphia, PA 19103
(215) 732-9444

Furniture and decorative arts of the late 19th and early 20th centuries. Although not strictly Victorian, the furniture represents a period of somewhat fanciful design, especially the French Art Nouveau movement, 1895–1910, which coincided with Victoriana.

MARGARET B. CALDWELL
147 East 82nd Street
New York, NY 10028
(212) 472-8636

Fine 19th-century furniture and decorations. By appointment only.

J. CANTO
1416 Center Street
Bethlehem, PA 18018
(215) 866-1649

Fine-quality oil paintings and 18th- and 19th-century furniture. By appointment only.

CAPE ISLAND TRADING COMPANY
609 Jefferson Street
Cape May, NJ 08204
(609) 884-6028

Furniture, accessories, and restored gas and early electric fixtures with an emphasis on Victoriana in a shop located in a livery stable (ca. 1875).

MICHAEL CAREY, INC.
107 Spring Street
New York, NY 10012
(212) 226-3710

Mission oak furniture and accessories by Stickley, Roycroft, Grueby, Fulper, Frank Lloyd Wright, and Dirk Van Erp.

CAVERN VIEW ANTIQUES
4678 Bannerville Road
R.D. #1, Box 23
Howes Cave, NY 12092
(518) 296-8052

All aspects of American Victoriana including sets of chairs, small tables, stools, bamboo pieces, etc., and decorative accessories such as mirrors, frames, ironstone, and glassware. (Bed and breakfast accommodations in an 1872 Italianate home furnished with Victorian antiques.)

CEDARBURG WOOLEN MILL
W62 N580 Washington Avenue
Cedarburg, WI 53102
(414) 377-0345

Located in a building dating from the early 1900s, with original tin ceiling and walls, this shop features antique quilts, rag rugs, lace curtains, and fabrics. Complete quilt restoration/repair service available. (Daily tours of the working mill are available, and on the second floor of the shop vintage looms are on display.)

THE CHATELAINE SHOP
Box 436
Georgetown, CT 06829
(203) 226-5501

Sophisticated 19th-century furniture and decorative accessories, with a specialization in American silverplate of the last half of the century and Gothic Revival furniture. Also ebonized furniture from the 1880s and 1890s. By appointment only.

CHERCHEZ
862 Lexington Avenue
New York, NY 10021
(212) 737-8215

Victorian lace and bed/table linens dating from 1830 to 1890. Also, Victorian ceramics for the table as well as 19th-century dressing-table accessories and silver.

CIRCA ANTIQUES, LTD.
374 Atlantic Avenue
Brooklyn, NY 11217
(718) 596-1866

Mainly American Victorian furniture and some late-19th-century lighting and accessories.

CITY BARN ANTIQUES
362 Atlantic Avenue
Brooklyn, NY 11217
(718) 855-8566

American mid- to late-Victorian lighting and decorative arts; some furnishings. Call first during the week. Open weekends.

RITA ENTMACHER COHEN
Box 708
Closter, NJ 07624
(201) 768-0058

Victorian decorative arts and furnishings, including English willow ware, 19th-century samplers, Nailsea rolling pins, beadwork. By appointment.

THE COLLECTED WORKS
905 Ridge Road
Wilmette, IL 60091
(312) 251-1120

American late-Victorian wicker furniture, in original condition and finish, as well as some pieces that have been painted.

THE COLLECTOR'S COTTAGE
30 Chestnut Ridge Road
Montvale, NJ 07546
(201) 573-9339

Antiques and out-of-print books on antiques, decorative arts, and related subjects.

CORNUCOPIA
R.D. Box 2108
Edge Road
Syosset, NY 11791
(516) 921-4813

Rare books and ephemera—subjects include cooking, needlework, gardening, domestic history, and related subjects. Focus on printed material of the 19th and 20th centuries. Call for an appointment.

THE COTTAGE GARDEN
3166 Maple Drive, NE, Suite 200
Atlanta, GA 30305
(404) 233-2050

This shop specializes in the accessories needed to complete a room. Specialties include silver tussie-mussie holders, dried-flower arrangements, garlands, lavender and rose topiaries, nosegays, flowerpots, and cachepots. Also available: fresh flowers of exceptional quality.

LA CRÈME DE LA CRÈME
3 Ferncliff Terrace
Montclair, NJ 07042
(201) 509-1899

Fine furniture, especially rosewood and inlaid. Specializes in American Rococo and Renais-

sance Revival: Belter, Meeks, Jelliff, Roux, Hunzinger, Henkels, and Pottier and Stymus. By appointment.

D

MARY K. DARRAH DECORATIVE ARTS AND ANTIQUES
33 Ferry Street
New Hope, PA 18938
(215) 862-5927

Furniture and accessories, needlework, paisleys, and china from the 1880s as well as American Gothic Revival, rustic and Aesthetic Movement furniture. Always a selection of period slipper chairs and needlepoint.

DICK'S ANTIQUES
670 Lake Avenue
Bristol, CT 06010
(203) 584-2566

American furniture, lighting, decorative arts, and accessories from 1840 to 1910. Features sideboards and servers, china closets, sets of press-back chairs, chifforobes, cylinder desks, glassware, clocks, and marble-topped furniture. Repair service is available in chair caning, refinishing, and restoration, including curved cabinet glass for furniture.

D'ORSI DESIGNS
147 Ford Street
Sudbury, MA 01776
(508) 443-8435

Antique needlepoint and Aubusson cushions and footstools. All cushions have antique or semiantique trim.

THE DRAWING ROOM
221 Spring Street
Newport, RI 02840
(401) 841-5060

High-quality Aesthetic Movement furniture; lighting and decorative arts of interest to those creating a historically accurate environment.

RICHARD AND ELLEN DUBROW ANTIQUES
Box 128
Bayside, NY 11361
(718) 767-8758

Fine- and museum-quality furniture from 1840 to 1890 and appropriate decorative arts. Special emphasis on cabinetmakers such as Herter, Meeks, Roux, Belter, and Hunzinger, as well as Wooten desks.

E

ERIE STREET ANTIQUES
131 Erie Street
Jersey City, NJ 07302
(201) 656-5396

Carved and ornate American Victorian furniture from the mid to the late 19th century. Armoires, bedroom sets, and overmantel mirrors a specialty.

F

FARM RIVER ANTIQUES
26 Broadway
North Haven, CT 06473
(203) 239-2434

High-quality American Victorian furniture from the 1840s to the 1890s. Also accessories of superior quality from the period. Shop is located in a renovated firehouse.

MIMI FINDLAY ANTIQUES
177 East 87th Street,
    Suite 404
New York, NY 10128
(212) 410-5920

High-quality American furniture from 1830 to 1890, as well as lighting, decorative arts, and accessories. Design advice for period rooms and collections available. By appointment.

LAURA FISHER ANTIQUE QUILTS AND AMERICANA
1050 Second Avenue, Gallery 57A
New York, NY 10022
(212) 838-2596

Textiles and decorative accessories: American antique quilts, woven coverlets, vintage bed coverings and home furnishing textiles. Specialty includes paisley and kashmir shawls. Also samplers, needlepoint, and fabric pictures as well as hand-painted mirrors, tramp art, and some folk-art items.

FLAPPER ALLEY, LTD.
1518 North Farwell Avenue
Milwaukee, WI 53202
(414) 276-6252

Late-Victorian antique clothing and accessories. Also fancy bed and table linens.

FLORIAN PAPP, INC.
962 Madison Avenue
New York, NY 10021
(212) 288-6770

Fine Aesthetic Movement and Arts and Crafts styles of furniture.

FLY-BY-NIGHT GALLERY
714 Wells Street
Chicago, IL 60610
(312) 664-8136

Art Nouveau and Arts and Crafts styles of furniture as well as related decorative accessories.

PATRICIA FUNT GALLERY
50½ East 78th Street
New York, NY 10021
(212) 772-2482

Victorian collectibles and accessories of all kinds, including snuff boxes, dolls, toys, games, miniature architectural collectibles, and paper ephemera.

G

GARGOYLES, LTD.
512 South Third Street
Philadelphia, PA 19147
(215) 629-1700

Architectural antiques of all periods—especially mid-to-late 19th century. Advertisement signs and memorabilia, eclectic country furnishings, stained-glass windows and doors.

J. GARVIN MECKING, INC.
72 East 11th Street
New York, NY 10003
(212) 677-4316

Furniture and decorative accessories of all sorts with an emphasis on the Victorian.

THE GASLIGHT COMPANY
107 Market Street
Lewes, DE 19958
(302) 645-4755

American lighting from the early and late 19th century, including gas, gas-electric, and early electric appliances.

GONZALES ANTIQUES, INC.
2313 Calvert Street, NW
Washington, DC 20008
(203) 234-3336

Antique chandeliers of every description and sconces. Restoration services for important vintage lighting available. Call for appointment.

GRAND ILLUSIONS
26 Barton Hill
East Hampton, CT 06424
(203) 267-8682

Kaleidoscopes a specialty. All high quality and made of brass, wood, and leather, as well as models from the 1880s.

STUART GRANNEN'S
ARCHITECTURAL ARTIFACTS
3759 North Ravenswood
Chicago, IL 60613
(312) 348-0622

American architectural artifacts such as mantels, stained and beveled glass, lighting, doors and hardware, woodwork, bathroom fixtures, decorative ironwork and fencing. Specializes in terra-cotta and carved-stone ornaments.

H

HARVEY ANTIQUES
1231 Chicago Avenue
Evanston, IL 60202
(312) 866-6766

Fine jewelry of the Victorian era; most 14k to 18k with gemstones.

HERITAGE LACE & LINEN
9 Pond Road
Rowayton, CT 06853
(203) 656-1555

Lace, linen, embroidered textiles, and christening gowns, all from the Victorian era. Specializes in locating items for clients. Appraisal service available.

PETER HILL, INC.
Maplewood Manor/Nicholas Road
East Lempster, NH 03605
(603) 863-3656

Fine 19th-century furniture and decorative arts with documentation. Also, will perform search for specific items on request.

HILLMAN/GEMINI ANTIQUES
743 Madison Avenue
New York, NY 10021
(212) 734-3262

Antique toys and mechanical banks a specialty. Also, 19th-century American paintings, carvings, and hooked rugs. Some painted 19th-century American furniture.

I

ILLUSTRIOUS LIGHTING, INC.
1925 Fillmore Street
San Francisco, CA 94115
(415) 922-3133

Specializes in restored American and Continental lighting and accessories from the period of 1840 to 1940. Also, working gaslights and gaslights that have been converted to electricity. All restoration done on premises.

IMPORTED LACES UNLIMITED
339 Washington Street
Wellesley Hills, MA 01860
(617) 235-6812

Fine American and Continental 19th-century lace, including curtains, tablecloths, and bedding.

J

JAMES II GALLERIES, INC.
15 East 57th Street, 6th Floor
New York, NY 10022
(212) 355-7040

Entire range of fine Victoriana, including jewelry, silver, silverplate, brass, porcelain, glass, furniture, and other decorative arts. Major emphasis on mid-Victorian period.

MARGOT JOHNSON, INC.
18 East 68th Street, Suite 1A
New York, NY 10021
(212) 260-3185

Fine museum-quality 19th-century American antiques specializing in Aesthetic Movement pieces, furniture designed by Herter and other prominent cabinetmakers.

RUTH E. JORDAN
Meridale, NY 13224
(607) 746-2082

American brilliant-cut glass, 1885–1910. Mail order only.

THE JUMPING FROG
161 South Whitney
Hartford, CT 06103
(203) 523-1622

Nineteenth-century books and ephemera with an emphasis on transportation, Americana, biography, cooking, photography, literature, and travel.

JUSTINIAN ANTIQUES
205 Waring Road
Syracuse, NY 13224
(315) 446-8752

American and English Victorian glass, pottery, and china. Specialty includes art glass, satin glass, and pattern glass, as well as flow-blue china, Staffordshire, transferware, and art pottery.

K

KATY KANE
38 West Ferry
New Hope, PA 18938
(215) 862-5873

Antique clothing from the Victorian period as well as 19th-century quilts and textiles.

KENTSHIRE GALLERIES, LTD.
37 East 12th Street
New York, NY 10021
(212) 673-6644

High-quality and unusual furniture and decorative accessories in a wide range of Victorian styles.

KING, INC.
Tracey Road
Northeast Harbor, ME 04662
(207) 667-7113

Authentic antique American wicker furniture and furnishings from the late 19th and early 20th centuries.

THOMAS H. KRAMER, INC.
805 Depot Street
Commerce Park
Columbus, IN 47201
(812) 379-4097

Furniture and accessories, mostly mid-Victorian. English, American, and some Continental pieces.

KURLAND-ZABAR
19 East 71st Street, Suite 1A
New York, NY 10021
(212) 517-8576

Furniture, silver, and decorative arts, including textiles, ceramics, lighting, and metalware. Most pieces are from 1840 to 1940 and include Gothic Revival, Egyptian Revival, Renaissance Revival, and Aesthetic Movement as well as some Arts and Crafts. Designers and makers featured include Tiffany & Co., Kimbel & Cabus, Christopher Dresser, C. R. Ashbee, and C. R. Mackintosh. By appointment.

L

LACE BROKER
252 Newbury Street
Boston, MA 02116
(617) 267-5954

Antique laces, linens, and fabrics from the Victorian era.

LACEWORKS/ANN LAWRENCE
ANTIQUES
250 West 39th Street,
**   8th Floor**
New York, NY 10018
(212) 302-4036

An extensive collection of antique lace, including clothing, bed linens, pillows, tablecloths, all from the mid- to late-Victorian era. By appointment.

ROBERT LANG
771 Matianuck Avenue
Windsor, CT 06095
(203) 688-9661

Specializes in the world of fly-fishing and related antiques. Includes lines of vintage fishing tackle; antique rods, reels, lures; books; and related ephemera. By appointment only.

LATHAM-KEARNS
205 East 16th Street, #5B
New York, NY 10003
(212) 505-9127

Decorative arts and furniture from the Aesthetic and Arts and Crafts movements. By appointment.

M

MANCHESTER ANTIQUE MALL
116 East Main Street
Manchester, MI 48158
(313) 428-9357

An extensive inventory of formal and country Victorian furniture. Also, 19th-century paintings, prints, jewelry, porcelain, and parlor lighting. Emphasis on Empire, Renaissance Revival American furniture.

SUSAN D. MASCOLO
Box 304
Brodheadsville, PA 18322
(717) 992-3574

Silverplated hollowware, including tea/coffee sets, cake baskets, tureens, flower holders, centerpieces, and gold-filled jewelry. American mid- to late-Victorian pieces a specialty. All silverplate in perfect condition, not restored; all polished by hand. By appointment.

RICHARD McGEEHAN
Box 181
Bedford Hills, NY 10507

High-style American and English furniture, silver and decorations, 1820–1900. Also specializes in period interiors. By appointment.

McGREGOR & COMPANY
2635 Steel Street
Houston, TX 77098
(713) 521-3307

Nineteenth-century fine-quality American antiques and decorative furnishings.

SCHMUL MEIER, INC.
15 Main Street
Tarrytown, NY 10591
(914) 332-1310

High-quality textiles, fabrics, needlepoint; decorative accessories such as valances, portieres, tiebacks. All from mid- to late-Victorian period.

BETTY MESSINGER
Box 293
Granby, CT 06035
(203) 379-2171

Extensive collection of 19th-century ephemera organized into categories such as advertising, photography, die cuts, valentines, and holiday cards, in a variety of sizes. By appointment.

MOLLY'S/GRANDMOTHER'S VINTAGE CLOTHING PROMOTIONS
Box 3400
Framingham, MA 01701
(508) 877-8863

Clothing and jewelry, accessories, textiles, rugs, samplers, books, prints, and ephemera related to fashion.

MONGERSON WUNDERLICH GALLERIES
704 North Wells Street
Chicago, IL 60610
(312) 943-2354

Victorian birdcages, beaded purses, tramp art, English beaded footstools, pillows, etc. All objects with a Victorian flair done from 1880 to 1930.

NORMAN MULVEY ANTIQUE TELEPHONES
1 Rudolf Lane
Norwalk, CT 06851
(203) 847-1155

Specializes in accessories and antique telephones from 1877 to 1895. Restoration and wiring services available.

N

LILLIAN NASSAU, LTD.
220 East 57th Street
New York, NY 10022
(212) 759-6069

Original works of art by Louis C. Tiffany, including lamps, glass, paintings, and pottery. Decorative objects from the late 19th century.

NEWEL ART GALLERIES, INC.
425 East 53rd Street
New York, NY 10022
(212) 758-1970

Furniture, lighting, and textiles, both American and Continental, from the Victorian period. Includes a large collection of Belter, Meeks, and bamboo furniture as well as papier-mâché inlaid mother-of-pearl furniture and other decorative pieces.

THE NEW YORK GAME PRESERVE
160 West 34th Street
New York, NY 10001
(212) 465-0570

Extensive collection of high-quality 19th-century games and related ephemera. Also features exceptional toys from the Victorian decades. Specialty includes puzzles and games by American manufacturers. By appointment.

REBECCA NOHE ANTIQUES
419 North Cascade Avenue
Colorado Springs, CO 80909
(719) 635-8425

Antique lace and linens as well as heirloom clothing and vintage accessories. Antique bridal veils, wax orange-blossom headpieces, and very fine handmade laces are specialties. Offers both American and Continental items from the mid- to late-Victorian era.

O

OSTER-JENSEN ART & ANTIQUES
86 Birch Hill Road
Locust Valley, NY 11560
(516) 676-5454

American, English, and Continental furniture, Victoriana, and accessories. Early- and mid-Victorian pieces a specialty.

P

PARENTEAU STUDIOS ANTIQUES GALLERY
230 West Huron Street
Chicago, IL 60610
(312) 337-8015

Museum-quality 19th-century American and Continental furnishings and accessories, including large-scale textiles, mirrors, and cast-iron and terra-cotta statuary.

BARBARA C. PAULSON, ANTIQUARIAN PAPER
Allen Coit Road
Huntington, MA 01050
(413) 667-3208

High-quality Victorian greeting cards, 19th-century trade cards and die cuts, as well as exceptional early children's books. By appointment.

PERRISUE SILVER
Box 2353
Princeton, NJ 08540
(609) 924-2141

Rare American 19th- and 20th-century silver. Hollowware and flatware a specialty. By appointment.

DAVID L. PETROVSKY
2785 Old Yorktown Road
Yorktown Heights, NY 10598
(914) 245-4294

Nineteenth-century American furniture and decorative arts of high quality. Call for appointment.

PHILIP W. PFEIFER
LE CABINET SCIENTIFIQUE
Lahaska Antique Court
Routes 202 and 263
Buckingham Professional Building
Buckingham, PA 18912
(215) 794-7333

Nineteenth-century decorative accessories, including match safes, snuffboxes, crystal, brass, games, and scientific instruments (nautical, medical, dental, astronomical). Drawing and drafting tools a specialty.

THE PURPLE PIG
49A South Main Street
Centerville, OH 45458
(513) 436-3158

Nineteenth-century country antiques from America and Europe as well as antique accessories.

R _____

THE RABBIT PATCH
604 Main Street
Portland, CT 06480
(203) 342-4364

Antique textiles and accessories: girls' dresses, linens, lamps, fine china, hats, buggies, sewing baskets, pictures, parasols, pull toys, and weathervanes. Most items have an emphasis on childhood.

DAVID RAGO
Box 3592, Station E
Trenton, NJ 08629
(609) 585-2546

Exceptional 19th-century American Arts and Crafts–style furniture, art pottery, lighting, and accessories. By appointment.

GENE REED
75 South Broadway
Nyack, NY 10960
(914) 358-3750

Victorian furniture with a focus on bamboo furniture of all styles.

REGENCY ANTIQUES
1719 West 45th Street
Kansas City, MO 64111
(816) 531-4740

American furniture, jewelry, accessories, and decorative arts. Specializes in sterling silver pieces. Matching service available for Victorian silver, silverplate, hollowware, and flatware.

REMEMBER WHEN
114 Main Street
Cold Spring, NY 10516
(914) 265-2424

Nineteeth-century furnishings and accessories, with an emphasis on Victorian furniture and tableware.

REPEAT PERFORMANCE ANTIQUES
377A Atlantic Avenue
Brooklyn, NY 11217
(718) 867-7980

Specializing in high-quality, original-finish furniture with an emphasis on bedroom, dining room, and parlor pieces as well as interior fretwork and stained glass—Rococo Revival, Renaissance Revival, and other styles.

RETRO FASHIONS
Box 353
River Edge, NJ 07661
(201) 261-7514

Fashion textiles and accessories as well as antique lace and linen. Bridal and home accessories. By appointment.

ROBINSON MURRAY III
150 Lynde Street
Melrose, MA 02176
(617) 665-3094

Nineteenth-century rare American books on unusual topics. Appraisals and library consultation services available upon request. By appointment only.

STELLA RUBIN ANTIQUES
12300 Glen Road
Potomac, MD 20854
(301) 948-4187

Specializes in quilts and textiles from 1830 to 1930, with an emphasis on American items of high quality.

RUFFLES
2048 Utica Square
Tulsa, OK 74114
(918) 743-1600

Victorian accessories, including bedding, lighting (custom French shades with French ribbons), lace tissue boxes, gloves, framed botanicals in vintage book paper, and ribbon.

S _____

SCARBOROUGH AND COMPANY
Box 637
Wilton, NH 03086
(603) 673-3800

Accessories such as ruffled pillows, sachet hearts, mini pillows, and pomanders in the Victorian style.

SCENTSIBLE PLEASURES
P.O. Box 718
Amherst, NH 03031
(603) 672-2633

Decorative herbal wreaths and potpourri, true
to the Victorian period in contents and style.

SCHILLY & REHS, INC.
305 East 63rd Street
New York, NY 10021
(212) 355-5710

Large collection of 19th-century British paintings and fine-quality genre paintings by American and British artists of the Victorian era.

**SCHOOLHOUSE GALLERY AND
    ANTIQUES**
Route 251
Layton, NJ 07851
(201) 948-4505

Furniture, lamps, accessories, china, and majolica; antique Victorian frames with 19th-
century genre prints (animals and hunting
scenes).

JERI SCHWARTZ
555 Old Ridge Road
Stamford, CT 06903
(203) 329-9633

Fine 19th-century silver, smalls, and virtu.
Specializes in unusual items such as tussie-
mussie holders made of exquisite materials.
By appointment only.

SECOND CHANCE
40 West Main Street
Southampton, NY 11968
(516) 283-2988

Linen, jewelry, and decorative objects from the
late 19th century (1865–1900). Specializes in
vintage pillowcases, silver napkin rings, dressing-table accessories, china, and brass objects.

S. J. SHRUBSOLE CORP.
104 East 57th Street
New York, NY 10022
(212) 753-8920

Silver and jewelry, mostly early- to mid-19th-
century American and European.

**SOMETHIN' ELSE ANTIQUES &
    NEEDLE ARTS**
182 Ninth Avenue
New York, NY 10011
(212) 924-0006

Linen, laces, textiles, jet jewelry, and decorative arts. Specializes in framed laces, tapestries, needlepoint, and paisleys.

SOUTHAMPTON ANTIQUES
172 College Highway, Route 10
Southampton, MA 01073
(413) 527-1022

Large selection of American Victorian furniture, Rococo Revival to Eastlake periods.

STANLEY GALLERIES
2118 North Clark Street
Chicago, IL 60614
(312) 281-1614

Victorian furniture and furnishings, including
19th-century chandeliers, floor, table, and
desk lamps as well as wall sconces. Most fixtures from ca. 1840 to 1935.

BARBARA STEINBERG UNLIMITED
964 Lexington Avenue
New York, NY 10021
(212) 439-9600

Continental Victorian accessories include
magnifiers, toaster racks, inkwells, ashtrays,
and dressing-table objects.

**STINGRAY HORNSBY ANTIQUES
    AND INTERIORS**
5 The Green
Watertown, CT 06795
(203) 274-2293

High-quality furniture, decorative arts, and
accessories—American and Continental—
representing all 19th-century styles: Classical,
Empire, Gothic Revival, Egyptian Revival, Renaissance Revival, Modern Gothic, and Aesthetic Movement.

STUBBS PRINTS AND BOOKS
835 Madison Avenue, 2nd Floor
New York, NY 10021
(212) 772-3120

Books, prints, and ephemera from the 19th
century on such subjects as architecture, decorative arts, gardens, landscape architecture,
domestic arts (cooking, housekeeping man-
uals), etiquette, textiles, fashion history, design, and crafts. An exceptional source for
unusual prints and original vintage designs.

SUNSET ANTIQUES, INC.
22 North Washington
Oxford, MI 48051
(313) 628-1111

Domestic architecture a specialty. Features
antique as well as custom-designed entry
doors, sidelights, and windows. Nineteenth-
century oak, cherry, and mahogany fireplace
mantels. Specializes in period designs.

SUPERLATIVES
234 Nichols Road
Kansas City, MO 64112
(816) 561-7610

Early-Victorian furniture, decorative accessories, and artwork. Interior-design services
available by appointment.

SUSSEX ANTIQUES
Box 796
Bedford, NY 10506
(914) 241-2919

Vintage bed and table linens, lace christening
gowns, and whites. Top-quality textiles, American and English, from the mid- to late-Victorian era. By appointment only.

SWEET NELLIE
1262 Madison Avenue
New York, NY 10128
(212) 876-5775

Victorian accessories for the home. Specializes
in American textiles, quilts, lace, and tabletop
accessories.

T

THAXTON & CO.
780 Madison Avenue
New York, NY 10021
(212) 988-4001

Dining-table accessories such as epergnes, coffeepots, tea sets, salts, serving pieces, vases, etc. Specializes in mid- to late-Victorian era, mostly European and some American.

ISAIAH THOMAS BOOKS AND
PRINTS
980 Main Street
Worcester, MA 01603
(508) 754-0750

Unusual 19th-century books and prints of high quality. Call for appointment.

TRANSATLANTIQUES
Court Road
Bedford Village, NY 10506
(914) 234-7220

Fine 19th-century linens and lace as well as an assortment of Victorian silver, china, crystal, and small furnishings.

N. P. TRENT ANTIQUES
3729 South Dixie Highway
West Palm Beach, FL 33405
(407) 832-0919

Nineteenth-century Americana and furniture, including wicker chairs, tables, and assorted accessories. Wicker armchairs a specialty.

TUDOR ROSE ANTIQUES
28 East Tenth Street
New York, NY 10003
(212) 677-5239

Early-, mid- and late-Victorian silver, American and Continental. Specializes in sterling-silver picture frames, dressing-table items (perfume bottles), crystal and silver jars, rouge pots, and hollowware. Unusual serving pieces also found here.

U

UNITED HOUSE WRECKING
535 Hope Street
Stamford, CT 06906
(203) 348-5371

Furniture, lighting, and all types of accessories, including brass, glassware, mantels, doors, and stained glass. All decades of the Victorian era in architectural artifacts, gingerbread, hardware, and plumbing fixtures.

UPSTAIRS, DOWNSTAIRS
Houghton Point North
North Swanzey, NH 03431
(603) 352-7231

Collectibles such as British royalty commemoratives, antiques and other Victorian-era accessories. Specializes in china, tea services, and unique decorative plates and boxes. By appointment.

V

VALLEY HOUSE
182 Birch Hill Road
Locust Valley, NY 11560
(516) 671-2847

Decorative accessories, chairs, tables, lamps, shades, and needlepoint rugs displayed in complete room settings that include other American and European Victorian items.

VAUGHN'S ANTIQUES
630 Hudson Street
New York, NY 10014
(212) 243-0440

Furniture and lighting fixtures from the Victorian period. Specializes in American rolltop desks and gas chandeliers.

VICTORIAN ATTIC
Main Road Mattituck
Box 831
Mattituck, NY 11952
(516) 298-4789

Antique wicker and limited edition of wicker pattern book reproductions. Also, silverplate and hollowware from Empire to turn-of-the-century styles. Both American and Continental. By appointment only.

VICTORIAN BELLE INTERIORS
Bell and Route 306
Chagrin Falls, OH 44022
(216) 884-0228

American Victorian furniture from 1840 to 1900. Chairs, loveseats, tables, lamps, desks, whatnots, halltrees, and mirrors made from walnut, rosewood, and mahogany. Restoration services for upholstery, including tufting and buttoning.

THE VICTORIAN LADY
76 Main Street
Talcottville, CT 06066
(203) 649-3106

Victorian silverplate dining accessories specializing in figurative napkin rings, cake baskets, pickle castors, coffee and tea services, butter dishes. Mostly American late-Victorian pieces. By appointment only.

VINTAGE TRADITIONS
20 Waterloo Avenue
Berwyn, PA 19312
(215) 647-9286

Quality jewelry and accessories, furniture, and porcelain from the mid- to late-Victorian periods. Some American.

W

WACKY WICKER WORKS
976 Mayfield Road
Chester Land, OH 44026
(216) 729-3395

American Victorian furniture such as chairs, rockers, settees, tea carts, chaises, dining tables, and chairs. Specializes in restoration of furniture as well.

HARVEY WEINSTEIN, INC.
22 Halifax Drive
Morganville, NJ 07751
(201) 536-4467

Tiffany lamps as well as Pairpoint, Puffy, Galle & Daum, and Handel lamps a specialty.

WHIPPOORWILL
3519 Broad Street
Chamblee, GA 30341
(404) 455-8357

Accessories, furniture, and decorative arts from the 1890s and early 20th century. Oak furniture, brass and iron beds, wicker and country furniture, and accessories from the Victorian decades.

WICKER GARDEN
1318 Madison Avenue
New York, NY 10128
(212) 410-7000

Antique wicker furniture and accessories including picture frames, lamps, hand-punched lampshades, antique mirrors, baby bedding, Victorian cribs, and other nursery items.

THE WICKER LADY
1197 Walnut Street
Newton Highlands, MA 02161
(617) 964-7590

Antique wicker furniture and distinctive accessories dating from 1890s through the turn of the century. Also elegant reproduction wicker and hand-painted Victorian-style furniture.

THE WICKER PORCH
13 North Water Street
Nantucket, MA 02554
(508) 228-1052

Victorian wicker and cast-iron furniture. Also decorative objects dating from the 1890s. The shop is located in a Gothic Revival house (ca. 1860).

WHIMSY
Scott's Corner
Pound Ridge, NY 10576
(914) 764-5400

Quality selection of 19th-century quilts, needlepoint pillows, tole trays, mirrors, and assorted Victorian furniture. Also informal antiques and accessories.

ELAINE WILMARTH
5717 Sir Galahad Road
Glenn Dale, MD 20769
(301) 464-1567

Featured items include Marseilles spreads, Victorian bed linens, table toppers, banquet linens, 19th-century pillow shams, assorted vintage lace collars, antique fashions, and hallmarked English sterling. By appointment.

WINDWARD ANTIQUES AND GIFTS
214 East Main Street
Flushing, MI 48433
(313) 659-1166

Specializes in Victorian English silver, jewelry, and linens.

WOLDMAN & WOLDMAN
Box 19839
Alexandria, VA 22320
(703) 548-3122

Furniture, lighting, porcelain, paintings and graphics, gilt and bronze decorative hardware, mostly American, 1810–1845, encompassing the early Victorian years. Objects in the Gothic Revival style as well. Quality chairs, marble-topped pier tables, worktables, dining room tables, ottomans, sofas, looking glasses.

WOODEN NICKEL ANTIQUES
1400-1414 Central Parkway
Cincinnati, OH 45210
(513) 241-2985

Architectural antiques such as doors, mantels, stained glass, lighting, mirrors, and hardware. Mostly mid-Victorian.

WOODSBRIDGE ANTIQUES
15 Haines Road
Bedford Hills, NY 10507
(914) 241-8660

Arts and Crafts, Mission furniture and accessories. Call for appointment.

THOMAS K. WOODWARD
AMERICAN ANTIQUES AND QUILTS
835 Madison Avenue, 2nd Floor
New York, NY 10022
(212) 794-9404

American 19th-century quilts and country furnishings. Specializes in 19th-century reproduction woven carpets as well. Rag rugs and patchwork quilts available.

THE WRECKING BAR OF
ATLANTA, INC.
292 Moreland Avenue, NE
Atlanta, GA 30307
(404) 525-0468

Architectural items such as fretwork, corbels and brackets, columns, mantels, and doors. All American and late 19th century in style.

WURLITZER-BRUCK
60 Riverside Drive
New York, NY 10024
(212) 787-6431

Musical instruments, prints and paintings with musical subjects, music stands, and music autographs. Nineteenth-century objects from America and Europe. By appointment only.

Z _____

SHELLEY ZEGART QUILTS
12-Z River Road
Louisville, KY 40207
(502) 897-7566

American quilts from the 19th century, including a wide selection of graphic indigo and whites, red and green appliqués, chintz quilts, and Victorian crazy quilts.

Credits and Acknowledgments

I'd like to express my thanks to the following for their energies, expertise, and hard work on this book: my always-excellent agent Deborah Geltman; the first-class team at Clarkson Potter, most especially my editor Lauren Shakely for the care and sensitivity with which she has consistently guided this project, and art directors Howard Klein, Karen Grant, and James Holcomb for their elegant design. Thanks, too, to photographer Edward Addeo, whose gifts of artistry, interest, judgment, and friendship all made working on this book a very special pleasure; and to my editorial assistant Carol Coleman for her unflagging enthusiasm and superb organization. Without the encouragement, comments, and critiques from dear friend Jody Shields and my sisters, Jody Leopold and Stacy Leopold— and help of special nature from my mother and my husband—completing this book would have been a lot more difficult. Finally, very special thanks and more to my dear friend and invaluable associate Joanne Cassullo— for her research, her fine work on the directory, her insights and obsessiveness, and her encouragement. She joined this project at its very beginnings, and nurtured it with me, becoming a Victoriana convert and collector— and cherished friend—in the process.

In addition, my appreciation to the collectors, curators, homeowners, antiques dealers, experts, and others who participated in this project in various ways: Marcie and Richard Miller, Sharon Abroms, Ed and Debbie Mc-Cord, Georgia Shapiro, Chuck and Doris ("Sam") Soucy, Jeanne Golly, Dennis Rolland, Anne and Rob Smith, Don Liles, Don Van Derby, Alan Clendenon, LaDel and Ivy Clendenon, Ralph DuCasse, Tom Roberts, Clem and Claire Labine, Barry Harwood, Kevin Statin, Neita and Jean-Marie Blondeau, George Sanborn, Stuart White, Jim Rogers, Margot Johnson, Marvin and Honey Leopold, Andrea Swenson, Bruce Bradbury, Paul Pilgrim, Gerald Roy, Ian and Maggie Berke, Paul Roberts and Cathy Ferron, John Burrows, Dan Diehl, and Starr Ockenga, with very special thanks to collector Richard Reutlinger, for his continuing graciousness, hospitality, and goodwill. I'd also like to acknowledge Nancy Novogrod for first getting this project off the ground.

Particular thanks to Lisa and William Benau, whose hospitality and collections were enjoyed at their lovely Victorian Inn on the Park in San Francisco (pages 6–7; 96; and 98, top), as well as a special thank you to Lisa for her grandmother's hauntingly beautiful photo that appears on page 33. I'd also like to acknowledge Tudor Rose Antiques, New York City, for their exquisite 19th-century sterling accessories (pages 11; 25, bottom; 28, top and bottom; and 29, bottom); Andrea Swenson for her collection of vintage tins (page 22); Marjorie Parrott Adams for providing splendid examples of Victorian mourning ephemera (page 40) and vintage sea mosses; and curator Barry Harwood for his extraordinary collection of Aesthetic-era porcelain and silver (pages 64, 66, 67, 69, 70, 92). For beautiful flowers, I'd like to thank James Goslee, (pages 144–149); and Darva Stapleton and Ryan Gainey of the Potted Plant, Atlanta, Ga. (page 138).

In addition to those objects that appear in the "Portfolio of Homes," the objects on the following pages belong to the following collectors.

Pages 1, 42, 44–45, 48, 54, 59 top, 74, 75 bottom left and right, 76, 78, 87 top left, 90, 91, 111: collection of Richard Reutlinger.

Pages 8, 49, 55, 61, 84, 103, 206: collections of John Raymond and Philip Rudko.

Pages 29, 98 bottom: antique purses, collection of Rita Baron-Faust.

Pages 32, 75 top, 85, 89, 99 bottom right, 109 top left, 151: collection of Chuck and Doris Soucy.

Pages 35, 46 top, 57 bottom, 71, 72–73, 86, 93: The Pilgrim/Roy Collection.

Pages 37: tussie-mussie, courtesy of Mrs. Rush Hannon Graves.

Page 40, Queen Victoria's funeral leaf: collection of Joanne L. Cassullo.

Page 41: Alan and LaDel Clendenon.

Pages 43 top, 77 top, 79 top, 87 (excluding top left), 88, 204: collection of Jean-Marie and Neita Blondeau.

Pages 43 bottom, 57 top, 99 bottom left, 101 bottom: collection of Ed and Debbie McCord, The Shelmont Inn, Atlanta, Ga.

Pages 46 bottom, 53, 58, 77 bottom, 82, 95, 205: collection of Marcie and Richard Miller.

Pages 51, 60, 102, 108 top, 116: collection of Anne and Ron Smith.

Pages 64, 66, 67, 70, 92: The Thornside Collection, Germantown, N.Y., at the home of Marvin and Honey Leopold.

Page 69, top row, center: The Pilgrim/Roy Collection.

Pages 79 bottom, 83 top, 114, 119: collection of Jim Rogers.

Page 81, clockwise from top left: collections of Don Van Derby and Don Liles, Marcie and Richard Miller, Jim Rogers, The Pilgrim/Roy Collection, and Marcie and Richard Miller.

Pages 83 below left and right, 120: collection of Don Liles and Don Van Derby.

Page 94, clockwise from top left: collections of Chuck and Doris Soucy, Soucy, Tom Roberts and Ralph DuCasse, Marcie and Richard Miller, Roberts and DuCasse, Roberts and DuCasse.

Pages 100, 101 top, 110: collection of Tom Roberts and Ralph DuCasse.

Page 106, top row: collections of Marcie and Richard Miller, Miller, Ralph DuCasse and Tom Roberts; center: Chuck and Doris Soucy, Soucy, anonymous; bottom: The Pilgrim/Roy Collection.

Page 107, top row: collections of Marcie and Richard Miller, Jeanne Golly, Richard Reutlinger; center: Richard Reutlinger, Jim Rogers, Richard Reutlinger, Ralph DuCasse and Tom Roberts.

Page 109 right, 118: Alan and LaDel Clendenon.

Page 112 top row, left to right: collections of Tom Roberts and Ralph DuCasse, Georgia Shapiro, Georgia Shapiro, Jim Rogers; row 2: Georgia Shapiro; row 3: (left) Georgia Shapiro, (right) Jim Rogers; row 4: Jim Rogers.

Page 115: collection of Georgia Shapiro.

Page 121: collection of Sharon Abroms.

Pages 144–149: collection of Jeanne Golly. Decorating, Jeanne Golly, Margot Johnson, Dennis Rolland; Portuguese needlepoint rug, Stark Carpet Corp.

Page 150, 154–157: collection of George Sanborn, The New York Game Preserve, New York City, at the home of Joanne L. Cassullo.

Page 224: collection of John and Jane Stubbs.

Selected Bibliography and Notes

In portraying Victorian Americans and their attitudes toward objects and collecting, I've relied on a range of sources. In addition to articles in antiques and design/decorative arts publications on specialized subjects, original sources—19th-century books, magazines, newspapers, personal journals and diaries, paintings, illustrations, and photographs—have proved invaluable in piecing together the puzzle of 19th-century life. Letters, labels, postcards, calendars, even dance cards, menus, and other century-old ephemera, as well as the popular fiction already referred to in the text, were also illuminating for a more personal, individual perception of how the Victorians saw themselves and their time.

Victorian treatises on the home and its decoration provided a basic blueprint for standards of acquisition and arrangement. Among them, well-known classics like *The House Beautiful* by Clarence Cook, first published in 1878; Charles Locke Eastlake's *Hints on Household Taste in Furniture, Upholstery and Other Details* (1872); and an excellent and all-inclusive book, *The Household: A Cyclopedia of Practical Hints for Modern Homes,* edited by May Perrin Goff in 1881. Also, *The American Woman's Home* (1869) by Catherine E. Beecher and Harriet Beecher Stowe; *Hill's Manual of Social and Business Forms* (1884); Harriet Prescott Spofford's *Art Decoration Applied to Furniture* (1878); and Robert W. Edis's *Decoration and Furniture of Town Houses* (1881). In addition, I found helpful information (and enjoyable reading) on domestic needlework in Addie E. Heron's *Fancy Work for Pleasure and Profit* (1905) and in reprints of *Household Elegancies* by Mrs. C. S. Jones and Henry T. Williams (1875) and *The Lady's Handbook of Fancy Needlework,* first published during the 1880s.

An even more worthwhile and beguiling exploration, though, for customs, dictums and quaint trends, curious specifics, for the

genuine tang and taste of the era, has been to delve into 19th-century magazines of all kinds —*The Ladies' World, The Delineator, Woman's Home Companion, The Ladies Home Journal,* to name just a few. Wherever possible I've cited isolated issues in the text. Each citation, however, represents the perusal of dozens of sister issues before arriving at an accurate portrayal of the attitude toward objects in the home. *Godey's Lady's Book* during the 1850s and 1860s; *Harper's Bazaar* during the 1870s, 1880s, and 1890s; *Peterson's Magazine* (bound, 1866); and many issues of *Harper's Weekly* (for their extraordinary graphic illustrations) were most valuable. Less obviously useful but somewhat interesting to check out were Victorian "annuals" and albums—bound collections of essays, musical compositions, poetry, verse, fiction, and other writings, with proud "embellishments" (illustrations, that is) of various sorts. The choice of what an annual like *The Ladies Wreath and Parlor Annual* (ca. 1855) featured and the tone and manner of expression, convictions, and sentiments depicted in the essays and the fiction, were further clues to Victorian mind, mood, and spirit.

Because I view objects and their display as an expression of social and cultural mores, I've also made a peripheral study of books on manners and behavior. These etiquette guides include *Our Deportment, or the Manners, Conduct and Dress of the Most Refined Society* by John H. Young (1882); a 1916 edition of Emily Holt's *Encyclopedia of Etiquette, A Book of Manners for Everyday Use,* originally published in 1901; *Good Morals and Gentle Manners for Schools and Families* by Alex M. Gow (1873); *Polite Life and Etiquette,*

or *What Is Right and the Social Arts* by Georgene Corry Benham (1891); *The Bazar Book of Decorum* (1870); *Manners and Rules of Good Society, A Compendium of the Proper Etiquette to be Observed on Every Occasion* (no author), issued by The New York Book Company in 1913; *Manners and Social Usages* by Mary Elizabeth Sherwood (1884); and Timothy Titcomb's *Letters to Young People, Single and Married* (1858). Works by the prolific Marion Harland, who wrote the *Common Sense in the Household* series, *Eve's Daughters, or Common Sense for Maid, Wife and Mother* (1882), and *Everyday Etiquette, A Practical Manual of Social Usages* (by Marion Harland and Virginia Van de Water) (1905), as well as issues of *The Home-Maker, A Monthly Magazine Edited by Marion Harland,* were also helpful.

Works by contemporary historians and experts I've consulted for background have included Katharine Morrison McClinton's *Collecting American Victorian Antiques* (1978); *A Documentary History of American Interiors from the Colonial Era to 1915* by Edgar de N. Mayhew and Minor Myers, Jr. (1980); *Authentic Decor: The Domestic Interior, 1620 to 1920* (1984); *American Manners and Morals* by Mary Cable and the editors of American Heritage (1969); *Victorian Silver* by Larry Freeman (1967); *Confidence Men and Painted Women: A Study of Middle-Class Culture in America, 1830–1870* by Karen Halttunen (1982); *The Strange Life of Objects* by Maurice Rheims (1960); *Victorian Things* by Asa Briggs (1988); and my own *Victorian Splendor, Re-creating America's 19th-Century Interiors* (1986). Finally, I most strongly recommend the hard-to-find but delightful *Decorative Art of Victoria's Era* by Frances Lichten (1950).

Index

Abroms, Sharon, 134
"accomplishments," 59–60
Aesthetic Movement, 13, 62–63, 68, 69, 71, 93, 110, 147, 176, 198, 200, 218, 220
alabaster, 68, 122
Albert, Prince, 174, 175, 177
Allen Brothers, 166
American Homestead series (Currier and Ives), 50
American Woman's Home (Beecher and Stowe), 54
angel motifs, 158, 196
animals, animal motifs, 126, 140, 142, 169, 170, 192, 195, 196, 198, 200
prints of, 77, 79
see also taxidermy
antimacassars (tidies), 62
arrangement and display, 88–115
of art, 77, 79, 90, 104, 110, 113, 158
asymmetry and, 93
clustering and, 93–94, 102, 109
drapery and, 98, 99, 108, 109–110
furniture for, 104, 106–109
lighting and, 96
of mantelscapes, 96–99
of tabletops, 99, 101, 102
of vignettes, 101, 102, 104
of wallscapes, 110, 113
Art Nouveau style, 125, 177
asymmetry, 93
autograph albums, 76

Bareness, Victorian distaste for, 65, 93, 94, 110
barometers, 186
bathrooms, 24, 107, 195
beadwork, 60, 85, 102, 220, 221
on canes, 163
on pillows and cushions, 38, 140, 185
Beardsley, Aubrey, 125
beauty, Victorian ideal of, 16
bedrooms, 25, 29, 209, 213, 214, 222
Aesthetic-style, 218, 220, 222
Russian-style, 220, 221
beds, 57, 213, 220, 222
Beecher, Catherine E., 54, 62
bell jars, 82, 196
Belter, John Henry, 64
Benham, Georgene Corry, 80
Berke (collector), 168–170
billiard rooms, 142, 143
birds, bird motifs, 163, 169, 173, 176–177
bookmarks, 27
books, 15, 20, 34
bindings of, 200, 202
collecting of, 79–80, 101, 129, 200, 202
covers of, 16, 80
botanical prints, 76, 77, 79
bowls, 39, 58, 134
boxes, 192, 194
collar, 47, 76, 175
pill, 102
sailors' valentines, 86
Brooks, Thomas, 169
Bryan, William Jennings, 163

butler's pantry, 106
buttonhooks, 19
Byron, Joseph, 129

Cabinet cards, 76
cabinets, 106, 107, 108, 132, 147, 156, 194, 202
Renaissance Revival, 166–170
calling card holders, 98, 169, 170
calling cards, 16, 76, 202
candleholders, 93
candlesticks, 97, 98, 196
candy containers, 191, 192, 196
canes and walking sticks, 162–165
Carey, Rosa N., 67
carpets, 36, 57, 64, 65, 173
castor sets, 214
ceilings, 148, 166, 173, 185, 209, 210
centerpieces, 21
chairs, 41, 102, 144, 147, 213
baby, 194
fashion and, 38, 125
Gothic Revival, 13, 15
Renaissance Revival, 166, 185
rocking, 47, 213, 220
Rococo Revival, 13, 26
chandeliers, 185
cherished objects, 39
chests, 77
children, 16, 20, 24, 46, 200
see also games; toys
china, 41, 66, 67–69, 71, 85, 209
Andrée Putman, 146
blue-and-white, 68, 69
display of, 108, 132
painting of, 60
Clendenon, Alan, 129
Clendenon, Ivy, 129
Clendenon, LaDel, 129
clocks, 63, 77, 96–97, 169, 212, 216, 221
clothing, 214
furnishings and, 38, 108, 109
see also dresses
clustering, 93–94, 102, 109
collar boxes, 47, 76, 175
collecting
early, 24, 29
of exotica, 140–143
in "grand manner," 122–127
mistakes in, 25, 27
modern mix in, 144–149
motivation for, 10, 13
nostalgic, 129–133
period-perfect, 204–223
romantic-style, 134–139
stages of, 25
"trading up" in, 25
collecting, by Victorians, 52–87
art and, 77, 79
books and, 79–80
china and, 67–69, 71
contemporary appreciation of, 113
fads and, 74–75
foreign items and, 68, 98
glass and, 71, 74
images and patterns and, 65
insecurity and, 76–77
mantelscapes and, 97–98
opulence and, 63–64
ornamentation and, 64–65
souvenirs and, 71, 82, 85–87
Colonial Revival, 207, 211, 216
commemoratives, 87, 174, 175, 177, 192
commodes, 220, 222
conversation, 50, 80

Cook, Clarence, 62, 80, 97, 104
cords, 13, 180
pictures hung on, 112
courtship, 76, 79
craft pieces, use of term, 27
Crystal Palace Exhibition (London) (1851), 64
Crystal Palace Exhibition (New York) (1853), 58
cupboards, 106, 108–109
cups, 38, 174, 175
Currier & Ives, 50, 182
cushions, 144, 147, 185

Daguerreotypes, 218
dance cards, 36, 195
Davis, Richard Harding, 38
daybeds, 144, 147
Decorator & Furnisher, 98
department stores, 58
desk accessories, 28
desks, 166, 186, 191, 202
dining rooms and areas, 20–21, 47, 50, 125, 132, 214
informal, 140, 166
Renaissance Revival, 166, 168, 185
dishes, 21, 41, 69, 132
see also cups; plates
doilies, 62
dolls, 195
doors, 20, 222
Downing, A. J., 77, 79
drapery, 98, 99, 108, 109–110, 126, 220
for mantels, 98, 110
for tables, 126, 129, 216
drawing rooms, 185, 186
Dresser, Christopher, 173, 176
dressers, 29, 30, 94, 107, 108, 134
dresses, 16, 34
baby's, 192, 195, 214
du Maurier, George, 68

Easels, paintings on, 79
Eastlake, Charles Lock, 62
Edward VII, King of England, 42
Empire style, 13, 213
Encyclopedia of Etiquette (Holt), 90
engravings, 76, 77, 79, 86
étagères, 13, 50, 104, 211
etiquette, 88, 90
exotica, Victorian, 140–143

Fads, 74–75, 158, 218
fairing, 85
family background and breeding, 77, 216, 218
fancywork, 54, 59, 60, 62
see also specific items
Fancy Work for Pleasure or Profit (Heron), 62
fans, 74, 173, 213, 214, 220
Field, Marshall, 146
"50 Soldiers on Parade," 154
fireplace and mantel tiles, 13, 15, 99, 216
flatware, 65, 67
floors, 166, 209
fly-swatter machines, 34
footstools, 43, 102, 138, 147, 182
frames, 29, 43, 102
Friedrich, Wenzel, 147

furniture
for arrangement and display, 104, 106–109
golden oak, 24, 25, 29, 108
Grand Rapids, 166, 220, 222
horn, 13, 147
matching suites of, 74
in public vs. private rooms, 25
rosewood, 63, 125, 144, 202
toy, 97, 194
see also specific items and periods

Games, 154–157, 191, 192
Gentleman's Magazine, 65
gilding, 64, 65, 69
glass
cut, 58, 71, 168
peacock-patterned, 173
pressed, 57, 58, 71, 74, 85, 106, 132
window, 182, 186
Godey's Lady's Book, 82
Goff, May Perrin, 59, 79
Golly, Jeanne, 144, 146–147
Gothic Revival style, 13, 15, 213
"grand manner" collecting, 122–127
Grand Rapids furniture, 166, 220, 222
"green rooms," 140, 186
greeting cards, 76
guest rooms, 29

Hair art, 13, 82, 83, 97, 125
halls, 15, 47, 50, 90, 194, 212
vignettes in, 104
hand coolers, 34
hands, mannequin, 191, 196
Harper's Bazar, 47, 57, 108
Harrison, Benjamin, 60, 163
Harrison, Caroline, 60
"headache" bags, 16
headboards, 57
heaters, 34
herbs and spices, 16, 19
Heron, Addie E., 59, 62
Herter, Christian, 166, 170
Herter Brothers, 25, 144, 146, 147
Heywood Wakefield wickers, 134, 138
highboys, 211
Hints on Household Taste (Eastlake), 62
Holt, Emily, 90
Home, a Book for the Family Circle (Tweedie), 59
Home Art, a Journal Dedicated to Interior Decoration, 59
home-centered life, 42, 43, 47, 50
fashion-furnishing link and, 109–110
homesteading, 57, 58, 59
horn furniture, 13, 147
house-as-a-collection concept, 178–189
House Beautiful, The (Cook), 80, 101, 104
Household, The (Goff), 59, 79, 96, 99
Household Elegancies, 185
Hughes, M. V., 108–109

Images and patterns, Victorian love of, 65
industrialization, 58, 63
inventions, 34, 57, 58
Irvine, Keith, 182
ivory pieces, 27, 126, 194

Jackson, Zue, 202
Japanesque craze, 67, 69, 74, 79, 93, 218
Johnson, Margot, 147
jugs, 174, 177

Kitchens, 20, 24, 106, 196
knife rests, 71

Labine, Claire, 173, 176–177
Labine, Clem, 173, 176–177
lace, 16, 21, 101, 138, 161, 186
Ladies Home Journal, 74
Ladies World, 34, 71, 74
"lady's book," 59
lamps, 96, 98, 102, 129, 134, 158, 200
lampshades, 82, 96
Lee, Gypsy Rose, 122, 125
letters, physician's, 28
libraries, 80
light, 64, 79, 96, 129, 138, 148, 166
light fixtures, 125
Liles, Don B., 122, 126
Limoges dinner services, 21
linens, 19, 58
    see also specific types
lithographs, 63, 77, 80
living rooms, 148
    see also parlors
lofts, 190–197
Lorillard, Pierre, 42
Loudoun, J. C., 58
luncheons, "colored," 74

Machine-made goods, 34, 42, 47, 58, 220
magazines, 24, 57, 59
    see also specific magazines
magnifying glasses, 27
mahogany, 15, 63, 182, 211, 222
mail order, 16, 20, 34, 58, 222
majolica, 71
mantels, 15, 63, 79, 122, 185, 216
    animal heads over, 142
    drapery for, 98, 110
mantelscapes, 96–99, 180
maps, 76, 202
marble, 64, 68, 79, 107, 122, 182, 220
    drapery and, 98, 110
marriage, 25, 60
masculinity, 38, 80, 166
Meade, L. T., 90, 93
Meeks, Joseph, 64
memorials, 83, 126
menu ephemera, 21, 71
Miller, Marcie, 209, 212–213, 214
Miller, Richard, 209, 212–213, 214
Minton china, 209
mirrors, 69, 107, 122, 125, 222
modern-mix style, 144–149
Montgomery Ward mail-order catalogues, 16, 20, 34
mourning memorabilia, 40, 192, 195
"Mr. Cliverford's Strategy," 39
musical instruments, 77, 213
mustaches, 38

Napkin rings, 24, 71
napkins, 21, 24
nature, 57, 80, 82, 125, 196
    mantelscapes and, 99, 180
    wallscapes and, 113

needlework, 59, 60, 62, 182, 186, 214
    see also specific kinds
Neo-Grec style, 166, 168, 173
"Newport Luncheon, The," 71
New York Interiors at the Turn of the Century (Byron), 129
niches, 104, 108, 192
nostalgic collecting, 129–133
novelty, 50

Oak, 63, 98, 185, 218, 220, 222
    golden, 24, 25, 29, 108
"object lust," 34
objects, disguised, 74, 75, 191, 192
ornamentation, 94, 99, 198–203
    Victorian collecting and, 64–65
overmantel, 98–99

Paintings, 77, 79, 90, 209, 212
paisley, 109, 144
Parian ware, 71, 79, 98, 174
Parloa, Maria, 62
parlors, 13, 15, 25, 47, 63, 200, 211, 216, 218
    aesthetics and, 50
    in "grand manner," 122, 125
    peacock, 173, 176–177
    Renaissance Revival, 166
parlor sets, 13, 38, 200, 220, 222
patents, 34, 57
peacocks, peacock feathers, 173, 176–177
peddlers, 58
period-perfect collecting, 204–223
Perks, Benjamin, 173
Peterson's, 39
Philadelphia Centennial Exhibition (1876), 58, 63, 79, 85
Philips, Barbara, 21
phonographs, 218, 222
photo albums, 76, 134, 196, 200
photo cards, 75–76
photography, 13, 15, 16, 24, 43, 46, 50, 75–76, 90, 99, 101
pie safes, 134
pill boxes, 102
pillows, 15, 138, 140, 142, 144, 221
    needlework, 182, 186
pin cushions, 27, 74, 75
"pineapple" brackets, 122
pitchers, 98, 132, 158, 174
placemats, 21
plates, 57, 158, 174
plumes, 113
Poe, Edgar Allan, 65
Polite Life and Etiquette, What is Right and the Social Arts (Benham), 80
porcelains, 64, 65, 67, 93, 126, 164, 191, 221
Porcelli, Ernst, 173
porches, 43
portraits, 21, 46, 50, 77, 90
potpourri, 19
Pottier & Stymus, 144
Potts, Mary Florence, 34
prints, 76, 77, 79, 202
progress, 42, 74
prosperity, Victoriana and, 39, 41, 47, 58, 64
Punch, 68
purses, 98
Putman, Andrée, 146

Queen Anne Pattern Cabinet Secretary, 202
quilts, 93, 140, 148
quilt tops, 15, 16

Racks, 77
Raymond, John, 216, 218, 220, 222
Renaissance Revival style, 13, 15, 64–65, 108, 166–171, 185, 198, 213, 216
Robert Mitchell and Frederick Rammelsberg, Cincinnati, 168
rocking chairs, 47, 213, 220
Rococo floral themes, 67
Rococo Revival style, 13, 64, 122, 125, 166, 213
Rogers, James B., 140, 182, 186
Rogers Group, 104
Rolland, Dennis, 146
romanticism, Victorian, 134–139
rosewood furniture, 63, 125, 144, 202
Rothschild family, 122, 125
Roux, Alexander, 64
Rudko, Philip, 216, 222

"Sad iron," 34
St. Nicholas, 200
salesmen's samples, 30
Sanborn, George, 154
sconces, 186
scrap, 13, 30, 93, 158, 186
screens, 30, 77, 79, 140, 186
    candle or lamp, 185
sculpture, 77, 79, 122
Seale, William, 101
seaweed, pressed, 82
sentimentality, 42, 76, 86, 158–161
servers, 108
serving dishes, 69
Sèvres china, 67, 68
sewing, 54, 59, 60, 62, 214
    boxes, 192, 214
    machines, 47
shawls, paisley, 109, 144
shell art, 13, 29, 59, 83, 86
sideboards, 41, 50, 108, 147
silver, 19, 21, 25, 28, 63, 214
    display of, 108
    sterling, 58, 71
silverplate, 58, 71, 169, 170, 196, 214
    motifs of, 198, 200
sitting rooms, 140
slipper chairs, 41
slippers, 60, 74, 85
Smith, Anne, 158
Smith, Ron, 158
smoking sets, 129
sofas, 166, 185
soup tureens, 170
souvenirs, 71, 82, 85–87, 140, 158, 218
Spofford, Harriet Prescott, 62
spoons, 71, 86, 158
    holders for, 39, 158
Staffordshire figures, 122, 174
stair landings, square, 182
stereoscopes, 75
still lifes, tabletop, 99, 101
stools, 43, 102, 138, 147, 182, 213
storage bins, 15
stoves, 34, 58
Stowe, Harriet Beecher, 54, 62
studies, 186
"suffragettes," 194
sugar bowls, 39
sun rooms, 138

Tablecloths, 21
tables, 122, 166, 194, 200, 213, 218
    billiard, 143
    dining, 50, 185, 196
    drapery for, 126, 129, 216
    Pottier & Stymus, 144
tabletops, 99, 101, 102, 126, 161
tassels, 132, 180, 185, 192
taste, predicament of, 58–59
Tasteful Interlude, The (Seale), 101, 129
taxidermy, 80, 82, 191, 196
teapoys, 13, 27
telephones, 218
Tiffany pieces, 21
tiles, 79
    fireplace and mantel, 13, 15, 99, 216
timepieces, 57
    see also clocks
tins, 24, 175
Titcomb, Timothy, Esquire, 38
toy furniture, 97, 194
toys, 46, 154, 157, 194, 195, 196
    see also games
trade cards, 75, 202
travel
    improvement of, 58, 63, 71, 82, 85, 86
    photos and, 75–76
trunks, 140
Turkish corners, 74
tussie-mussie, 36, 195
Twain, Mark, 57
Tweedie, Rev. W. K., 59

Umbrella holders, 143
upholstery, 140, 144, 211

Valentines, 25, 47
    sailors', 86
Van Derby, Don, 122, 126
vases, 68, 69, 108, 158, 221
Victoria, Queen of England, 16, 40, 42, 87, 122, 200
    commemoratives for, 174–175, 177
Victoriana
    American, 27, 30
    directory of, 225–236
    etiquette, status, and social class and, 39, 41
    price increases in, 27
Victorian period
    historic background of, 36, 38
    images conjured by word, 38–39
    insecurity of, 76–77
    self-assurance of, 42
vignettes, 101, 102, 104, 192, 195

Wakefield, Heywood, 134, 138
walking sticks and canes, 162–165
wall niches, 104, 108
wallpaper, 36, 65, 200
walls, 148, 166
wallscapes, 110, 113
washtubs, 15
White, Stuart, 163–164
Wilde, Oscar, 62–63, 68, 146
windows, 138, 148, 166, 182, 186, 192
womanhood, Victorian, images of, 158–161
woodwork, 176, 209, 222
World's Columbia Exposition (1893), 58
Wounded Gaul, The (sculpture), 122

Zebra heads, 142